DIMITRI SALACHAS – KRZYSZTOF NITKIEWICZ

INTER-ECCLESIAL RELATIONS BETWEEN EASTERN AND LATIN CATHOLICS

A CANONICAL-PASTORAL HANDBOOK

English Edition

George Dmitry Gallaro

Originally published as *Rapporti Interecclesiali tra Cattolici Orientali e Latini.*
© 2007 – Pontificio Instituto Orientale

Canon Law Society of America
3025 4th Street, NE, Suite 111
Washington, DC 20017-1102

TABLE OF CONTENTS

PREFACE

It is a distinct pleasure to present to the English-speaking public. This canonical handbook on inter-ecclesial relations in the Code of Canons of the Eastern Churches and the Code of Canon Law of the Latin Church. This project is not intended only or even primarily for canon lawyers but has been conceived and developed first and foremost to meet the needs of the Catholic faithful who find themselves under the pastoral care of clergy of a Church *sui iuris* different from their own and for the parish priests and deacons who serve them.

Most pastoral ministers in North America and elsewhere have had the experience of Catholic faithful of another Church *sui iuris* as members of their parish community. In the not-too-distant past such situations have usually involved Eastern Catholics in Latin parishes – e.g., a Ruthenian Byzantine Catholic or a (Syro) Maronite Catholic family in a Latin (Roman) parish -- or an Eastern Catholic family in an Eastern Catholic parish of a different Church *sui iuris* – e.g., a Romanian Byzantine Catholic family in a Ukrainian Byzantine Catholic parish – all in places where there is no parish of their own Church *sui iuris*. This phenomenon, however, now frequently involves situations of Latin (Roman) Catholic faithful becoming full members of Eastern Catholic parishes.

These new situations pose significant challenges to the pastoral ministers in the parish, especially in light of the Vatican II's Decree on the Eastern Catholic Churches, *Orientalium Ecclesiarum* (November 21, 1964), and the subsequent implementation by the two codes, the *Codex Iuris Canonici* (January 25, 1983) and the *Codex Canonum Ecclesiarum Orientalium* (October 18, 1990). A better mutual understanding (*mutua ac meliore cognitione*) of the proper Church *sui iuris* membership of the Christian faithful will enrich the proper ritual patrimony to which they have a right and also secure the valid and licit reception of the sacramental mysteries in the parishes they attend to.

It is a sound sign of the vitality of the Eastern Catholic Churches *sui iuris* in North America and elsewhere and of the ecclesiological sensitivity of the clergy and committed laity that, more and more frequently, appropriate issues are being raised regarding the administration and reception of the sacramental mysteries. The subject of inter-ecclesial and inter-ritual disciplinary norms is not only timely but also relevant.

This project has come to fruition through the collaboration of many persons. First are the two professional authors, Rev. Dimitri Salachas and Rev. Krzysztof Nitkiewicz, of the Pontifical Oriental Institute in Rome; then the translator and editor of the English edition, Rev. George Gallaro, of the Byzantine Catholic Seminary of Saints Cyril and Methodius in Pittsburgh; and finally the Canon Law Society of America officers and staff. The text here presented is substantially that of the Italian authors, but the English translation has been a free one. When quoting canons, I have used the official CLSA translations (Latin Code, 1998 edition; Eastern Code, 2001 edition). A 'thank-you' goes to the Rev. Peter Waslo, of the Archeparchy of Philadelphia and Chairman of the Eastern Canon Law Committee of the Canon Law Society of America, and the Rev. Michael Skockri of the Eparchy of Newton, for reviewing the English type-script. Sr. Margaret Ann Andrako, of the Order of St. Basil the Great, offered her time and assistance in the careful compilation of the final work. Finally, Msgr. John Alesandro of the Diocese of Rockville Centre and chair of the CLSA Publications Advisory Board reviewed the text and helped in improving the final version. To them all, I am most grateful.

George Dmitry Gallaro
Byzantine Catholic Seminary
Pittsburgh, Pennsylvania

FOREWORD

Inter-ecclesial Relations between Eastern and Latin Catholics: A Canonical-Pastoral Handbook was compiled by the Reverend Fathers Dimitrios Salachas, consultor, and Krzysztof Nitkiewicz, under-secretary, of the Congregation for the Eastern Churches. Both are also professors at the Pontifical Oriental Institute of Rome. "Better mutual understanding" (*mutua ac meliore cognitione*) is the official mandate or charge to Catholics worldwide by the Second Vatican Council in its Decree on the Eastern Catholic Churches, *Orientalium Ecclesiarum* (n. 24), fittingly published on the ninetieth anniversary of the founding of the Congregation for the Eastern Churches and the Pontifical Oriental Institute by Pope Benedict XV in 1917.

The *Code of Canons of the Eastern Churches*, promulgated in 1990 by Pope John Paul II is part of the canonical discipline of the entire Church *pari passu* with the *Code of Canon Law* of the Latin Church (1983) and the Apostolic Constitution *Pastor Bonus* (1988). The canons of the Eastern code apply only to Eastern Catholic Churches with the exception that, if in regard to mutual relations with the Latin Church problems of interpretation arise between the two codes, it would become necessary on the practical level to refer to the entire corpus of canons.

Eastern Catholic faithful who have moved from their places of origin to western countries have found themselves living beside their Latin brothers and sisters and are often subject to the pastoral care of Latin bishops and pastors. Migrations need not in any way become a cause for alienation and a loss of identity for Eastern Catholics. The Second Vatican Council and the Holy Father are of one mind in reiterating the necessity for all Christian faithful to safeguard the precious treasure of their Church of origin. All Christian faithful: clergy, religious and laity, are to faithfully follow their proper tradition, acquire a greater knowledge of it, and observe it more perfectly.

Certainly this fact contributes to a greater mutual knowledge and enrichment for all. The Latin and Eastern traditions of the one Church of Christ constitute the patrimony of the universal Church, and this heritage, shining from the Apostles and coming through the Fathers, proclaims the divine unity in the Churches of the Catholic faith.

This pastoral handbook can be very helpful as a resource to Latin bishops and religious superiors who very often have to deal with the Eastern Christian faithful in the exercise of their responsibilities. Indeed, the Decree on the Eastern Catholic Churches exhorts the pastors of the Latin Church, who by reason of their office or apostolic ministry have frequent contact with Eastern Christians, to be carefully instructed in the knowledge and practice of the ritual, theology, law, teaching, history and spirituality of Eastern Christians, in keeping with the importance of the office they hold (OE 6).

This handbook aims at being of assistance in addressing the pastoral and canonical concerns of our Churches, and I am confident that all our Christian communities can receive some benefit from it. It will be particularly useful not only to bishops, presbyters and deacons, but also to students of theology, parish collaborators, and lay faithful.

It goes without saying that the two current codes continue to regulate inter-ecclesial and inter-ritual relations, even though experience testifies to the fact that the often-followed praxis does not always correspond to the norm. Therefore, this handbook, translated into English by Reverend Father George D. Gallaro, instructor of canon law and ecumenical theology at the Byzantine Catholic Seminary of Saints Cyril and Methodius of Pittsburgh, is enthusiastically welcomed with the hope of assisting in the practical solution of our pastoral concerns. May it also contribute to "a better mutual understanding" between the Latin and Eastern Churches *sui iuris* and be a source of unity for all Christians.

+ Basil Myron Schott, D.D.
Metropolitan Archbishop
Byzantine Catholic Church *sui iuris* of Pittsburgh
Chairman, Association of the USA Eastern Bishops

ABBREVIATIONS

AAS	*Acta Apostolicae Sedis*
AG	*Ad gentes*, Decree on the Missionary Activity of the Church, December 7, 1965
c.; cc.	canon; canons
CCC	Catechism of the Catholic Church, August 15, 1997
CCEO	*Codex Canonum Ecclesiarum Orientalium*, October 18, 1990
CD	*Christus Dominus*, Decree on the Pastoral Office of Bishops in the Church, October 28, 1965
CIC	*Codex Iuris Canonici*, January 25, 1983
Ap. Cons.	Apostolic Constitution
Ap. Ex.	Apostolic Exhortation
ED	Ecumenical Directory, Pontifical Council for Promoting Christian Unity, March 23, 1993
TCF	The Christian Faith in the Doctrinal Documents of the Catholic Church, edited by Jacques Dupuis, Bangalore 2004
LI	Instruction for Applying the Liturgical Prescriptions of the Code of Canons of the Eastern Churches, January 6, 1966
LG	*Lumen gentium*, Dogmatic Constitution on the Church, November 21, 1964
Encycl.	Encyclical Letter
no.; nos.	Number; numbers
OE	*Orientalium Ecclesiarum*, Decree on the Eastern Catholic Churches, November 21, 1964
OL	*Orientale Lumen*, Apostolic Letter on the Churches of the East, by John Paul II, May 2, 1995
OT	*Optatam totius*, Decree on Priestly Formation, October 28, 1965
PB	*Pastor bonus*, Apostolic Constitution on the Roman Curia, June 28, 1988
PO	*Presbyterorum ordinis*, Decree on the Ministry and Life of Priests, December 7, 1965
SC	*Sacrosanctum concilium*, Constitution on the Sacred Liturgy, December 4, 1963
UR	*Unitatis redintegratio*, Decree on Ecumenism, November 21, 1964

TERMS

SACRAMENTS OF INITIATION AND ASCRIPTION

Adaptation of Rite

All the Christian faithful are always bound to observe their own rite everywhere and to acquire a greater knowledge of it (CCEO c. 40). This obligation binds particularly the sacred ministers who celebrate the sacraments and the members of institutes of consecrated life (CCE cc. 40; 674; CIC c. 846, §2). However, when that proves impossible on a long term basis or there is a question of a spiritual benefit for the individual or others a papal indult of adaptation of rite is needed from the Congregation for the Eastern Churches. Cases of adaptation that occur more frequently are those obtained for entrance in a religious institute of another Church *sui iuris* and the incardination of an Eastern priest into a Latin diocese.

The above-mentioned indult gives the petitioner the faculty to be part of the liturgical, theological, spiritual and disciplinary patrimony of another Church, although always remaining ascribed to his own Church *sui iuris*. If, for some reason, the situation that prompted the concession should change, (e.g., when a religious is dismissed from a religious institute), the individual is required to observe his or her rite of origin.

Sacred ministers who are granted an adaptation of rite, even before being ordained, can celebrate the liturgy in either rite, the one of origin or that of adaptation.

See *Biritualism.*

Ascription of Adults to be Baptized to a Church *Sui Iuris*

Canonical Norm

Both codes prescribe that a candidate for baptism who has completed the fourteenth year of age can freely choose any Church *sui iuris*; he or she is then ascribed to that Church by virtue of the baptism received in it, with due regard for particular law established by the Holy See (CCEO c. 30; CIC c. 111, §2). As an example, the child of Eastern Catholic parents who has not yet been baptized and has completed fourteen years of age can freely choose the Latin Church, to which he or she is then ascribed by baptism. Likewise the child of Latin Catholic parents, not yet baptized who has completed fourteen years of age, can freely choose any Eastern Church *sui iuris,* to which he or she is then ascribed by baptism.

Recommendation

This norm is particularly important in mission territories. Canon 588 of the Eastern code, in dealing with catechumens, states: "Catechumens are free to be ascribed to any Church *sui iuris*, in accord with the norm of c. 30; however, care should be taken lest anything should be recommended that might prevent their ascription in the Church *sui iuris* more appropriate to their culture."

This norm is significant not only because to force or to induce with false pretences or to allure anyone to join the Catholic Church is strictly forbidden (CCEO c. 586; CIC c. 748, §2), but also in light of the inculturation of the Catholic faith. Undoubtedly, Eastern Catholic rites, differentiated by their culture and historical circumstances (CCEO c. 28, §1), are closely related to the manner of practicing the faith among the monotheistic peoples. This recommendation, which is not found in the Latin code, has particular importance in missionary work.

Ascription to a Church Sui Iuris of Children under 14 Years of Age

Ecclesiological-Juridical Principle

Every Catholic faithful is ascribed by virtue of baptism to the Latin Church or to an Eastern Church *sui iuris* in accordance with canonical norms (CCEO cc. 29-30; CIC c. 111, §1). However, it is not the liturgical rite of baptism that determines the canonical membership of a person in the Latin Church or an Eastern Church *sui iuris*, but the norm of the law. An individual, as a physical person, is not legally ascribed to a rite, but to a Church *sui iuris*.

Each Church *sui iuris* is established by the law itself as a juridic person (CCEO c. 921, §2) and is represented in the ecclesiastical and civil forum by the one who presides over it. Thus, if a minor child of Eastern parents has been baptized in a Latin parish, he or she is ascribed to the Church *sui iuris* of the parents; if a minor child of Latin parents has been baptized in an Eastern parish, he or she is ascribed to the Latin Church of the parents. In c. 683, the Eastern code expressly establishes the norm to be observed: "Baptism must be celebrated according to the liturgical prescripts of the Church *sui iuris* in which, in accord with the norm of law, the person to be baptized is to be ascribed." An exception from this norm can be justified by the lack of a priest of the same rite or by an indult granted from the Holy See.

Eastern and Latin Canonical Norm

Both codes establish the norm that to administer baptism in the territory of another requires permission (CCEO c. 678; CIC c. 862). However, the Eastern code, in c. 678 §1, adds: "This permission cannot be denied by a pastor of a different Church *sui iuris* to a priest of the Church *sui iuris* in which the person to be baptized is to be ascribed." In paragraph two of the same canon we read: "In places where there are not a few Christian faithful lacking a pastor of the Church *sui iuris* in which they are ascribed, the eparchial bishop should designate a presbyter of that Church, if it is possible, who should administer baptism."

These norms are missing from the Latin code, but they implicitly bind the Latin Church too. A problem could arise when the parents of the minor belong to different Catholic Churches, for example, one to the Latin Church and the other to one of the Eastern Churches. In this case, in compliance with the CCEO c. 29 §1, "A son or daughter who has not yet completed fourteen years of age is ascribed by virtue of baptism to the Church *sui iuris* to which his or her Catholic father is ascribed; or if only the mother is Catholic, or if both parents are of the same mind in requesting it, to the Church *sui iuris* of the mother, without prejudice to particular law by the Holy See."

The Latin code, in the corresponding c. 111 §1, states that, "Through the reception of baptism, the child of parents who belong to the Latin Church is enrolled in it, or, if one or the other does not belong to it, both parents have chosen by mutual agreement to have the offspring baptized in the Latin Church. If there is no mutual agreement, however, the child is enrolled in the ritual Church to which the father belongs."

On comparing Eastern code c. 29 §1 with Latin code c. 111 §1, it would seem that the Latin canon does not provide for the possibility of the ascription of a minor to the Eastern Church of the mother, while the Eastern canon does provide for it. But a careful reading of the Latin code comes to the conclusion that the same possibility is provided for. Latin canon 111 §1 does not seem to exclude the possibility that parents belonging to different Churches (Latin and Eastern) can by mutual agreement have the offspring baptized in the Eastern Church to which one of the two parents belongs. According to the norm of both codes, when the parents are not in agreement, their child is always ascribed into the Church of the father, whether he is Latin or Eastern. Consequently, there is ultimately no opposition between the two codes, even though the Eastern code emphasizes the preference of the father in determining the juridical state of the minor.

Baptism (celebration)

Baptism is celebrated according to the liturgical prescripts of the Church *sui iuris* in which the person to be baptized is to be ascribed (CCEO c. 683). A son or daughter of Eastern parents or of an Eastern father only must be baptized in the Church of the parents or the father. Whether or not the baptism has been celebrated in accordance with the appropriate liturgical rite (perhaps in a rite different from that of the parents of the person to be baptized), he or she is ascribed to the Church of the parents, in compliance with the Eastern code c. 29.

Minister of Baptism of Eastern Faithful

The sacrament of baptism in the Eastern Churches ordinarily is administered by a priest; the deacon is an extraordinary minister. In the Latin Church a deacon is an ordinary minister of the sacrament (CIC c. 861, §1). Accordingly, when the baptism of an Eastern faithful takes place in a Latin

Church, it must be administered by a priest (CCEO c. 677). Indeed, in places where a good number of the faithful have no parish priest of their own Church *sui iuris*, the local bishop should designate a presbyter of that Church, if it is possible, to administer baptism (CCEO c. 678).

Children Baptized in Danger of Death

A child, of Catholic or even of non-Catholic parents, who is in such critical condition that it can be prudently foreseen that he or she will die before reaching the use of reason is licitly baptized (CCEO c. 681, §4; CIC c. 868, §2). The need for the consent of the parents in order to baptize a child legitimately is a requirement of the natural law, for a child is by its very nature totally dependent on the parents until he or she can express his or her own will. By analogy, this also applies to children who have been adopted according to the norm of civil law: they are considered the children of the persons who have adopted them (CIC c. 110). In danger of death, the eternal salvation of a child prevails over parental rights, rendering licit the baptism of the child, whether of Catholic or non-Catholic parents, even apart from their consent.

Baptism of Children of Non-Catholic Parents on Their Request

The children of non-Catholic Christians are licitly baptized if their parents, or at least one of them or the person who legitimately takes their place, request it and if it is physically or morally impossible for them to approach their own minister (CCEO c. 681, §5). It is a rather common occurrence that non-Catholic Christian parents, especially Orthodox, for want of their own minister, ask the Catholic parish priest to baptize their son or daughter. The Eastern code in c. 681, §5 (no equivalent in the Latin code) allows the baptism of the child of non-Catholic Christians in this situation. In such a case, the non-Catholic parents have the primary obligation to see to the Christian education of the baptized child in their own Church.

Note that, for a child of Orthodox Christians to be licitly baptized in a Catholic Church, besides the free request of the parents, or at least of one of them or the person who legitimately takes their place, there must also be a physical or moral impossibility to approach their own minister. Today in nearly all western countries there are a number of Orthodox communities and Churches with legitimate pastors. Hence, Orthodox parents should always approach the Orthodox minister to have their son or daughter baptized, unless there is a real impossibility. Such impossibility may occur, for instance, among the Greek, Russian, Rumanian, and Albanian Orthodox because of a diversity of language, rituals and mentality. There may also be other reasons, including ethnic and political ones. In such instances, the request for baptism in a Catholic Church would seem legitimate.

Although this norm does not appear in the Latin code, it is implicitly in force *ex natura rei* in the Latin Church as well. In such a case, it is licit for the Latin parish priest to baptize the child, and, keeping in mind that chrismation/confirmation is administered jointly with baptism according to

Orthodox praxis, to confirm him or her, having received the faculty from the ordinary of the place to do so.

The child of Orthodox parents, although baptized in a Catholic Church, is ascribed to their respective Orthodox Church. The child could be received into the Catholic Church, respecting, however, the cautions found in c. 900 of the Eastern code: "§1. A person who has not yet completed his or her fourteenth year is not to be received [in the Catholic Church], if the parents are opposed to it. §2. If grave inconveniences are foreseen either to the Church or to the person from receiving such a person, the reception is to be deferred, unless there is imminent danger of death."

It is not prudent for a minor to be received in the Catholic Church, if the parents are opposed or the minor's reception will occasion serious hindrances to the Church or to the person, as well as to the ecumenical relationship between the Churches. In such case, reception should be postponed until the completion of the minor's fourteenth year of age.

If the parents are not opposed to it and the reception is not likely to cause serious inconveniences for the Church or the person, a minor may be legitimately received into the Catholic Church. In this case, for ascription to an Eastern Catholic Church *sui iuris* or the Latin Church, canon 35 of the Eastern code should be applied by analogy. Hence, the minor son or daughter of Orthodox parents must be ascribed to the Eastern Catholic Church *sui iuris* of the same rite of the parents. For example, a minor son or daughter of Orthodox Armenian parents, received legitimately into the Catholic Church, must be ascribed to the Catholic Armenian Church; he or she may be ascribed to the Latin Church only by indult of the Congregation for the Eastern Churches. Note, however, that to baptize this minor licitly and to receive him or her into the Catholic Armenian Church, one must have "a founded hope that he or she will be educated in the faith of the Catholic Church" (CCEO c. 681, §1, 1°; CIC c. 868, §1, 2°).

Baptism of Children of Non-Baptized Parents on Their Request

On occasion, Muslim parents may ask for the baptism of their minor son or daughter in the Catholic Church. This may arise when Muslim children attend a Catholic school and participate, with the consent of the parents, in classes of Catholic catechism. When the Muslim parents ask to have their child baptized in the Catholic Church, the baptism may not be refused if the child is sufficiently educated in the Christian faith. The Eastern code in c. 29, §2, 3° states: "If a person who has not yet completed fourteen years of age is of non-baptized parents, he or she (with the reception of baptism) is ascribed to the Church *sui iuris* to which belongs the one who has undertaken his or her education in the Catholic faith." Such a task is ordinarily assumed by the god-parents of baptism, but it could be another Christian person designated by the Muslim parents.

Record of Baptism

As far as the baptismal register of the parish is concerned, c. 689 §1 of the Eastern code prescribes that the parish priest of the place where the baptism has been celebrated must record accurately and without delay the name of the baptized, adding the minister, the parents, the sponsors, the place and date of birth and baptism and the annotation of the Church *sui iuris* to which the baptized person is ascribed (*see* also CCEO cc. 37; 296, §2; 689, §1).

The Latin code in corresponding c. 877 §1 does not mention the annotation of the Church *sui iuris* to which the baptized person is ascribed in compliance with the law. Canon 689 §1 of the CCEO fills this lacuna of the CIC: it applies equally to the Latin Church. Actually, the inclusion of the Church *sui iuris* to which the baptized person is ascribed, in compliance with the law, has a particular value for the legal status of every Catholic insofar as ascription may very well affect the validity of a marriage later on.

Baptism (Orthodox Churches and Protestant Ecclesial Communities)

Premise

Inter-ecclesial relations between the Catholic Church and the other Churches and Ecclesial Communities are based on the valid reception of the sacrament of baptism. All other sacramental and canonical acts - *communicatio in sacris*, mixed marriages, disparity of worship, dissolution of marriages, favor of the faith cases, reception of other Christians into the Catholic Church, sacramental sponsorship of non-Catholics at the baptism and confirmation of Catholics - in a word, all those privileges non-Catholics enjoy in the Catholic Church are contingent upon the validity of baptism. Catholic doctrine and its norm are established by the Decrees On ecumenism (UR 15-23), On the Eastern Churches (OE 27), and the Ecumenical Directory (ED 99 & 101).

Orthodox Baptism

Eastern Orthodox Churches have true sacraments, above all, by apostolic succession, the priesthood and the Eucharist. There is no doubt about the validity of baptism as conferred in the various Orthodox Churches: one need only establish the fact of the baptism. In these Churches the sacrament of chrismation/confirmation is properly administered to children as well as to adults by the priest at the time of the baptism. It often happens that no mention is made of chrismation in the canonical testimony of baptism; such omission is no reason to doubt that this sacrament was also conferred (ED 99a).

Protestant Baptism

With regard to Ecclesial Communities that arose at the end of the Middle Ages and in later centuries, baptism constitutes the sacramental link of union among all those who have been regenerated by it. As for the baptism conferred in the various Ecclesial Communities that use water and the invocation of the Holy Trinity, one should not automatically doubt its validity (ED 99b).

The Congregation for the Doctrine of the Faith, over the years, has officially declared the invalidity or non-existence of the baptism of various communities: e.g., the Apostolic Church, the Bohemian Free Thinkers, the

Christadelphians, the Church of Jesus Christ of Latter Day Saints/Mormons, Jehovah's Witnesses, the Reunification Church/Moonies, the Salvation Army, the Shakers, the Society of Friends/Quakers, the Swedenborgian Church, the Unitarians. One must also carefully take into account the risk of invalidity of baptisms conferred by aspersion, single or collective.

Doubt on the Validity of Baptism Chrismation of Other Churches and Ecclesial Communities

After the fall of communism in the Eastern European countries, a new situation arose in regard to Orthodox children legitimately adopted by Catholic families in the Western countries. Often one is faced with a lack of proof about the administration of baptism. The same may also happen with Orthodox planning to marry a Catholic party or enter into full communion with the Catholic Church. During the era of communism all religions were completely suppressed: no sacramental life was allowed. Clandestinity was the only way to receive baptism and the other sacraments.

In order to prove the administration of baptism and/or other sacraments in such cases, the declaration of one competent witness or even the declaration of the baptized person founded on solid arguments is sufficient. If there is some doubt that the person was in fact baptized or that the baptism was not validly administered and the doubt persists even after serious investigation, the sacrament may be conferred conditionally. The formula to be used in the conditional administration of baptism is the following: "If you are baptized, I do not baptize you; if you are not yet baptized, I baptize you, etc." (From fragments of the Letter of Pope Alexander III (+1181) to Pontius, the bishop of Clermont, of uncertain time), in Denzinger 758. When a prudent doubt exists as to whether a person has been baptized, and the doubt remains after a serious investigation, baptism is to be administered conditionally. The same norm applies to the sacrament of chrismation/confirmation (CCEO cc. 691 & 672, §2; CIC cc. 876 & 845, §2).

With regard to Protestant Christians, there should not be, as a rule, any reason to doubt the validity of baptism, unless in a particular case there is a serious reason to doubt the matter, the formula used, or the intention of the adult person baptized or of the minister who conferred the sacrament of baptism. If, after a careful investigation, a serious doubt persists about the proper administration of the baptism and it is judged necessary to baptize conditionally, the rite of conditional baptism is to be celebrated in private and not in public (ED 99d).

As for the sacrament of confirmation, in the present state of the relations with the Ecclesial Communities of the Reformation of the 16th century, there is, as yet, no agreement about the significance or sacramental nature or even the administration of this sacrament. Therefore, under present circumstances, persons entering into full communion with the Catholic Church from one of these Ecclesial Communities, are to receive the sacrament of confirmation according to the doctrine and the rite of the Catholic Church, before being admitted to Eucharistic communion (ED 101).

Biritualism

Biritualism is the faculty granted by the Holy See to an Eastern or Latin priest (bishop or presbyter) to celebrate the Divine Liturgy/Holy Mass and the Holy Sacraments according to the liturgical rite of another Church *sui iuris* as well as his own.

The Eastern code in c. 674 imposes the obligation to observe the proper liturgical rite in sacramental celebrations: "§1. In celebrating the sacraments, that which is contained in the liturgical books is to be observed accurately. §2. The minister should celebrate the sacraments according to the liturgical prescripts of his own Church *sui iuris*, unless the law establishes otherwise or he himself has obtained a special faculty." The Latin code in c. 846, §2 states that "The sacred minister is to celebrate the sacraments according to his own rite."

All bishops and presbyters should faithfully comply with this norm and, unless they are concelebrating the Holy Eucharist, should refrain from celebrating the Divine Liturgy/Holy Mass and the other Sacraments according to the liturgical rite of another Church *sui iuris*. In case of pastoral need, however, permission may be obtained from the Congregation for the Eastern Churches. The faculty of biritualism is normally granted for the spiritual good of the faithful, whether Eastern or Latin, for a period of time determined in the rescript; if needed, it may be renewed. The prior consent of both the Ordinary/Hierarch of the faithful in need of assistance and the petitioner's superior, as well as sufficient acquaintance with the rite on the part of the petitioner, are required for such a faculty to be granted.

Sacred ministers, who for some reason have received the adaptation of rite, are permitted to celebrate the Divine Liturgy/Holy Mass and the Holy Sacraments in their own rite as well as in that of their adaptation. The celebrant wears the liturgical vestments and insignia of the rite that he is officiating. The indult of biritualism is not needed to concelebrate the Divine Liturgy/Holy Mass, but each concelebrant should wear the liturgical vestments of his own Church *sui iuris* (CCEO c. 701; LI 57).

See *Adaptation of Rite.*

Catechumens

Canonical Norm

Catechumens are those who, under the influence of the Holy Spirit, ask by explicit choice to be incorporated into the Church and are joined to it in a special way. By this same desire and by leading a life of faith, hope and charity, they are united with the Church which already cherishes them as its own. The Church has a special concern for catechumens (CCEO c. 9; CIC c. 206).

The catechumenate is a very old institution. The Second Vatican Council restored, for the Latin Church, the catechumenate for adults and divided into various stages (SC 64). Today, in the Latin Church as well as the Eastern Churches, the Christian initiation of the adults begins with their entrance into the catechumenate and reaches its culmination with the joint celebration of the three sacraments of baptism, chrismation/confirmation, and Eucharist.

Through instruction and the first experience of Christian life, catechumens are to be initiated suitably into the mystery of salvation and introduced into the life of the faith, the liturgy, the charity of the people of God, and the apostolate (CCEO c. 587; CIC c. 788, §2). The Church invites catechumens to lead the evangelical life, introduces them into participation in the Divine Liturgy, the sacraments and the Divine Praises/Liturgy of the Hours, and already grants them various prerogatives proper to Christians (CCEO c. 9; CIC c. 206). When the period of the pre-catechumenate has been completed, those who have made known their intention to embrace faith in Christ are to be admitted to the catechumenate in liturgical ceremonies and their names are to be inscribed in the book designated for this purpose (CIC c. 788, §1). In the Latin Church this rite is found in the *Ordo initiationis christianae adultorum* (January 13, 1978) adapted by the conference of bishops and the special norms issued by it (CIC c. 851, §1; CCEO c. 682, §1). The funeral rites of the Catholic Church may be granted to catechumens (CCEO c. 875; ED 120).

Right of Catechumens to Choose Any Eastern Church Sui Iuris or the Latin Church

Catechumens are free to choose any Eastern Church *sui iuris* or the Latin Church in which they then are ascribed (CCEO c. 30; CIC c. 111, §2). The Eastern code in c. 588, assuring full freedom for catechumens to select any Church *sui iuris* (c. 30) in which to be ascribed, recommends that "care should be taken lest anything should be recommended that might prevent their ascription in the Church *sui iuris* more appropriate to their culture." This norm is important not only because it strictly forbids coercion or inducing anyone through improper practices or enticing them to join the Church and the Catholic faith (CCEO c. 586; CIC c. 748 §2), but also because it safeguards the pastoral perspective of the *salus animarum.*

Chrismation with Holy Myron (Confirmation)

Myron is a Greek word meaning a mixture of olive oil and balsam and other perfumes used for anointing persons during chrismation or confirmation. The Eastern Churches call the sacrament of confirmation by a traditional liturgical and canonical expression "chrismation with holy myron," that is, anointing with sacred chrism. Canon 7 of the First Ecumenical Council of Constantinople (381) describes the ritual of this sacrament as follows: "Those who embrace the true faith ... are first sealed or anointed with holy chrism on the forehead, eyes, nostrils, mouth, and ears. As we seal them we say: 'Seal of the gift of the Holy Spirit'". Holy myron is confected only by a bishop, without prejudice in the Eastern Churches to particular law, which reserves this power to the patriarch (CCEO c. 693). In the latter case, Eastern eparchial bishops constituted outside the boundaries of the patriarchal territory receive the holy myron from their respective patriarch.

Administration of the Sacrament

According to the tradition of the Eastern Churches, chrismation with holy myron must be administered to children or adults in conjunction with baptism, except in cases of true necessity, in which case, however, care is to be taken to have it administered as soon as possible. If the celebration of chrismation with holy myron is not done together with baptism, the sacred minister is obliged to notify the parish priest of the place where the baptism was administered (CCEO c. 695).

In the Latin Church the sacrament of confirmation is conferred on the faithful at about the age of discretion unless the conference of bishops has determined another age, or there is danger of death, or in the judgment of the sacred minister a serious cause suggests otherwise.

Minister of Chrismation

Chrismation with holy myron in the Eastern Churches is administered by a presbyter either in conjunction with baptism or separately (CCEO c. 694). Eastern presbyters can validly administer this sacrament to all the Christian faithful of any Church *sui iuris*, including the Latin Church. They licitly administer it only to the Christian faithful of their own Church *sui iuris*; when administered to the faithful of other Churches, they act licitly in regard to their own subjects, or those whom they licitly baptize in virtue of another title, or those in danger of death – always with due regard for the agreement entered between Churches *sui iuris* in this matter (CCEO c. 696, §3). When baptizing the faithful of the Latin Church, the minister is not required to confer it jointly with confirmation.

In the Latin Church, the ordinary minister of confirmation is a bishop; a presbyter provided with this faculty in virtue of universal law or the special grant of the competent authority also confers this sacrament validly (CIC c. 882). The Latin minister of confirmation validly administers this sacrament also to faithful of the Eastern Churches, according to the faculties extended to him. A frequent case is that foreseen by CCEO c. 916, §§ 4-5, when Eastern faithful are lacking their own parish priest and are entrusted to the pastoral care of a Latin ordinary or pastor. These sacred ministers are to follow the Eastern norm for the sacramental care of these Eastern faithful, in particular to administer chrismation with holy myron together with baptism. The Latin parish priest does not have to wait to confer this sacrament on Eastern faithful at the age of discretion or the age established by the conference of bishops. It goes without saying that he administers this sacrament according to the faculties given to him to care for the Eastern faithful in his area.

Registration of Chrismation with Holy Myron

When the celebration of chrismation with holy myron is not done together with baptism, the priest is obliged to notify the local pastor where the baptism was administered so that proper registration is entered in the sacramental book of the parish.

Since, in all the Eastern Churches, Catholic and Orthodox, the sacrament of chrismation with holy myron is regularly administered by a priest in conjunction with baptism, an Eastern parish generally annotates the chrismation in the register of baptisms in its archive. In the Latin Church the register of baptisms is kept separate from the register of confirmations. Consequently, it may happen that the canonical certificate of baptism of an Eastern faithful, Catholic or Orthodox, in a Latin church may make no mention of chrismation. This is not a basis for doubting that this sacrament was also conferred (ED 99a).

See *Sacraments of Christian Initiation.*

Eucharistic Communion of Children

Eastern Children in Latin Parishes

In the Eastern Churches "the sacramental initiation in the mystery of salvation is completed with the reception of the Divine Eucharist; therefore after baptism and chrismation with holy myron, the Divine Eucharist is to be administered as soon as possible in accord with the norms of the particular Church *sui iuris*" (CCEO c. 697). "Regarding the participation of infants in the Divine Eucharist after baptism and chrismation with holy myron, suitable precautions are to be taken and the prescripts of the liturgical books of the respective Church *sui iuris* are to be observed (CCEO c. 710).

Actually, a good number of the Eastern Catholic Churches follow the Latin praxis of administering first Holy Communion at the age of discretion. In any case, when Eastern Catholic parents in Latin territories who do not have their own (ritual) parish priest present their children for Eucharistic Communion, the Latin priest should comply with their request, taking into account recommended cautions.

See *Sacraments of Christian Initiation.*

Latin Children in Eastern Parishes

In the Latin Church: "The administration of the most Holy Eucharist to children requires that they have sufficient knowledge and careful preparation so that they understand the mystery of Christ according to their capacity and are able to receive the body of Christ with faith and devotion (CIC c. 913, §1). Consequently, in Eastern territories, because of the different Latin discipline, when Latin parents, who have no (ritual) parish priest of their own, present their children for first Holy Communion, the Eastern priest should comply with their request, after having taken into account the conditions required by the Latin code.

Eastern Non-Catholics Coming into Full Communion

Principle

Vatican II declares in the Decree on Ecumenism that, when those who have been validly baptized in non-Catholic Churches or Ecclesial Communities and spontaneously ask to enter full communion with the Catholic Church, either as individuals or as groups, "it is necessary to impose no burden beyond what is essential." (UR 18)

CCEO c. 897 affirms therefore that: "A member of the Christian faithful of an Eastern non-Catholic Church is to be received into the Catholic Church with only the profession of the Catholic faith, after a doctrinal and spiritual preparation that is suited to that person's condition." Since this constitutes a very delicate act, it is advisable to ascertain the weighty reasons why one asks for admission into the Catholic Church.

Competent Authority to Receive into Catholic Communion

The competent ecclesiastical authority to receive one into full communion is specified in CCEO cc. 898-899.

- For the individual layperson, it is the parish priest within the territory of his parish.
- In the case of a cleric, competency belongs to the local bishop and, if particular law so determines, to the patriarch as well. It is up to one of them to authorize a cleric to exercise the sacred ministry. According to well establish praxis, a non-Catholic priest is first received as a layman (*tamquam laicus*) and only after necessary updating is he ascribed to the new jurisdiction with the conferral of an office. If the cleric is to exercise the ministry in a rite different from that of his origin, e.g., the Latin rite, the Holy See must be petitioned for an accommodation of rite or bi-ritual faculties.
- A non-Catholic monk asking to be admitted into a religious institute, after having professed the Catholic faith, is required to go through the novitiate and make a religious profession again (CCEO c. 493 §2).
- An orthodox bishop can be received into the Catholic Church by the Roman Pontiff, a patriarch or a major archbishop with the consent of the synod of bishops of the patriarchal or major archiepiscopal Church or by a metropolitan *sui iuris* with the consent of his council of hierarchs. He will be able to exercise the power of governance only with the assent of the Roman Pontiff, head of the college of bishops.

Ecclesial Membership

CCEO c. 35, following the Decree on the Eastern Churches (OE 4), declares that: "Baptized non-Catholics coming into full communion with the Catholic Church should retain and practice their own rite and should observe it everywhere in the world as much as humanly possible." In the case of

Orthodox, the new Church of ascription shall be one of the twenty-one Eastern Catholic Churches *sui iuris*, the closest in its ritual approach. Protestants who enter into the full Catholic communion are to be ascribed to the Latin Church, since their Ecclesial Communities sprang from the Western/Latin tradition.

The rationale of this norm is mainly ecclesiological: full communion with the apostolic Church of Rome does not imply alienation or loss of the rite, understood as liturgical, theological, spiritual and disciplinary patrimony. Canon 35 was written with an ecumenical perspective in mind: to establish and to preserve communion one must "lay no greater burden than necessary" (Acts 15: 28). The Eastern Orthodox who joins the equivalent Eastern Catholic Church finds the surroundings in keeping with his/her Christian history and identity. That does not mean that he/she cannot continue to attend the Latin Church, even though it is desirable that he/she should be helped to uphold his/her own Church tradition.

Since the text of c. 35 does not explicitly specify if the norm is *ad validitatem* or *ad liceitatem*, one may infer that this is not an irritating law. Canon 32, §1, dealing with Catholics who desire to transfer validly to another Church *sui iuris*, requires the consent of the Holy See. Furthermore, insofar as legitimate ascription to another Church *sui iuris* constitutes the basis for the validity or liceity of certain juridic acts (e.g., the validity of a marriage or the licit admission to a religious institute of another Church *sui iuris*) one may conclude that c. 35 has a binding force, after all.

Sometimes, a baptized member of an Eastern non-Catholic Church who enters in full communion with the Catholic Church wants to be ascribed into the Latin Church. If so, one must, with the prior approval of the local Latin bishop, seek an indult from the Holy See, that is, the Congregation for the Eastern Churches. The canonical reason for such a petition must be serious, e.g., the spiritual well being of the petitioner or the unity of the family when the petitioner is married to a Latin spouse.

Incardination/Ascription of Clerics

Every cleric must be incardinated/ascribed as a cleric either to an diocese/eparchy, an exarchy/vicariate, a religious institute or a society of common life in the manner of religious, or to an institute or association that has obtained from competent authorities the right to incardinate/ascribe clerics (CCEO c. 357, §1; CIC c. 265).

As a rule, a cleric ascribed/incardinated to an Eastern eparchy or a Latin diocese is not permitted to transfer from his own particular Church to another. Ascription/incardination of a cleric into an ecclesiastical jurisdiction does not cease except by valid ascription/incardination to another (excardination) or by loss of the clerical state (CCEO c. 364; CIC c. 267, §2).

Eastern Clerics in Latin Dioceses

In accordance with the norm that a cleric is to serve the ecclesiastical territorial division for which he has been ordained, both codes, Eastern and

Latin, are consistent in stating that "a cleric who is solicitous about the universal Church, chiefly for the sake of evangelization, is not to be denied a transfer or move to another eparchy/diocese suffering from a severe shortage of clerics, so long as he is prepared and suitable for carrying out the ministry there (CCEO c. 361; CIC c. 271, §1).

From this perspective, an Eastern cleric could be destined for the service of a Latin diocese. But to legitimately exercise his ministry according to the Latin rite he needs an indult of adaptation to that rite or at least the faculty of bi-ritualism, both of which are granted by the Congregation for the Eastern Churches.

Likewise, when Eastern Christian faithful reside in Latin dioceses without their own hierarchy, the legislator contemplates the erection of personal parishes for them and the provision of pastoral care through the designation of pastors of their rite (CCEO c. 916, §§4-5; CIC cc. 383 §2; 1015, §2). Thus, a Latin diocesan bishop can incardinate in his own diocese an Eastern cleric and even ordain suitable Eastern candidates (CCEO c. 343) for the service of the faithful of the same Church *sui iuris*. The Holy See's permission must be secured for this provision (CCEO c. 748, §2; CIC c. 1015, §2).

When caring for Christian faithful who belong to a patriarchal or major archiepiscopal Church, the local Latin bishop should draw up a pastoral plan in consultation with the respective patriarch or major archbishop and inform the Holy See. If the patriarch or major archbishop disagrees for some reason or other, the matter should be referred to the Holy See (CCEO c. 193, §3).

Latin Clerics in Eastern Eparchies

An Eastern eparchial bishop can ascribe to his eparchy a Latin cleric to serve the Latin faithful who reside there. The cleric is to consider him as his proper hierarch by the special directives of the Holy See, as in the case of some Syro-Malabar eparchies outside of the State of Kerala in India or the eparchy of Piana degli Albanesi in Sicily, or simply by reason of domicile when the cleric does not have a hierarch of his own Church *sui iuris* (CCEO c. 916, §5). In order to confer sacred orders on a Latin candidate the hierarch needs the permission of the Holy See (CCEO c. 748, §2; CIC c. 1015).

Transfer from One Eparchy to Another of the Same Church Sui Iuris

For a licit transfer or move to another eparchy of the same Church *sui iuris*, just causes, such as the advantage of the Church or the good of the cleric himself, are required; permission, however, is not to be denied except for serious reasons (CCEO c. 365, §1; CIC c. 270). For a cleric, already ascribed to an eparchy, to transfer or move validly to another eparchy, he must obtain from his eparchial bishop a signed dimissorial letter and a letter of ascription signed by the eparchial bishop of the eparchy to which he wishes to be ascribed (CCEO c. 359; CIC c. 267, §1).

Transfer of an Eastern Cleric to a Latin Diocese

For a licit transfer or move of a cleric from an Eastern eparchy to a Latin diocese just causes, such as the advantage of the Church or the good of the cleric himself, are required; permission, however, is not to be denied except for serious reasons (CCEO c. 365, §1; CIC c. 270). For a cleric, already ascribed to an eparchy, to transfer or move validly to a Latin diocese, he must obtain from his eparchial bishop a signed dimissorial letter and a letter of incardination signed by the diocesan bishop of the diocese in which he wishes to be incardinated (CCEO c. 359; CIC c. 267, §1).

Moreover, if the particular law of a Church *sui iuris* so prescribes, the licit transfer or move to an eparchy of another Church *sui iuris* may require that the eparchial bishop releasing the cleric obtain the consent of the authority determined by the same particular law, that is, the patriarch, the major archbishop, or the Holy See (CCEO c. 365, §2). In this case, the transfer or move without such consent is invalid.

An Eastern cleric incardinated in a Latin diocese always remains ascribed to his own Church *sui iuris*; to exercise his ministry according to the Latin rite, he needs a special faculty from the Holy See, that is, the adaptation of rite or the indult of bi-ritualism (CCEO c. 674).

Transfer of a Latin Cleric to an Eastern Eparchy

For an incardinated Latin cleric to be ascribed validly to an Eastern eparchy, he must obtain from his diocesan bishop a signed letter of excardination and a letter of ascription signed by the eparchial bishop of the Eastern eparchy in which he desires to be ascribed (CIC c. 267, §1). In this case, the Latin cleric, though ascribed to the Eastern eparchy, always remains enrolled in the Latin Church; to exercise his ministry according to the Eastern rite he needs a special faculty from the Holy See, that is, the adaptation of rite or the indult of bi-ritualism (CIC c. 846). The Eastern code cautions the eparchial bishop not to ascribe an extern cleric to his eparchy unless he is convinced that the cleric has the aptitude to carry out the ministry, especially if the cleric comes from another Church *sui iuris*, including the Latin Church (CCEO c. 366, §1, 2°).

See *Adaptation of Rite; Biritualism.*

Sacraments of Christian Initiation

Unity of the Three Sacraments

The sacraments of baptism, chrismation, and the most holy Eucharist are interrelated in such a way that they are required for full Christian initiation into the mystery of Christ and the Church. This initiation into the mystery of salvation is brought to completion by the reception of the Divine Eucharist (CIC c. 842; CCEO c. 697). Although maintaining their own specificity, the sacraments of Christian initiation constitute an inseparable whole, in which chrismation completes baptism and the Eucharist is the fulfillment of the other two.

In the first centuries of the Church, Christian initiation had a great development with a period of catechumenate and a series of liturgical rites to be concluded by the celebration of the sacramental initiation. With the passing of time, the Christian initiation of children was celebrated also in a joint ceremony.

Liturgical Differences between East and West

"Today in all the rites, Latin and Eastern, the Christian initiation of adults begins with their entry into the catechumenate and reaches its culmination in a single celebration of the three sacraments of initiation: Baptism, Confirmation and the Eucharist. In the Eastern rites the Christian initiation of infants also begins with Baptism followed immediately by Confirmation and the Eucharist, while in the Roman rite it is followed by years of catechesis before being completed later by Confirmation and the Eucharist, the summit of their Christian initiation" (CCC 1233).

The Eastern code, upholding this ancient Christian tradition, states: "The sacramental initiation in the mystery of salvation is completed with the reception of the Divine Eucharist; therefore after baptism and chrismation with holy myron, the Divine Eucharist is to be administered as soon as possible in accord with the norms of the particular law of each Church *sui iuris*" (CCEO c. 697).

Undoubtedly, in the Eastern Churches the Christian initiation of children calls for a post-baptismal catechumenate. The praxis of the Eastern Churches emphasizes the unity of the work of the Holy Spirit *par excellence* and the fullness of incorporation of the baptized person into the sacramental life of the Church. The same praxis is also in effect in the Latin Church so far as adults are concerned (CIC c. 866). As for children, the three sacraments are spread out in time for practical pastoral reasons: "Confirmation is to be conferred on the faithful at about the age of discretion" (CIC c. 891); and "the most Holy Eucharist requires that children have sufficient knowledge and careful preparation so that they understand the mystery of Christ" (CIC c. 913, §1). The praxis of the Latin Church underlines more clearly the union of the baptized Christian with the bishop as guarantor of the "one, holy, catholic, and apostolic Church."

Christian Initiation of Eastern Faithful Entrusted to Latin Priests

When Eastern Christians are entrusted to the pastoral care of a Latin bishop or pastor (CCEO c. 916, §§4-5), the norms of the Eastern code are to be followed in serving them. Traditionally, chrismation with holy myron must be administered in conjunction with baptism, except in a case of true necessity, in which case, however, care is to be taken to have it administered as soon as possible" (CCEO c. 695). In Eastern Churches, sacramental initiation into the mystery of salvation is completed with the reception of tne Divine Eucharist; therefore, after baptism and chrismation, the Divine Eucharist is to be administered as soon as possible in accord with the norms of the particular law of each Church *sui iuris* (CCEO c. 697). Regarding the participation of infants in the Divine Eucharist after baptism and chrismation, suitable precautions are to be taken and the prescripts of the liturgical books of the respective Church *sui iuris* are to be observed (CCEO c. 710).

Consequently, Eastern Christian faithful can validly receive the sacrament of chrismation even from Latin presbyters who have been granted such a faculty. Furthermore, when Eastern parents present their children to Latin priests or deacons for Holy Communion, the children should receive it, even though the discipline of the Latin Church is different. Obviously, this should take place with due pastoral sensitivity in order to avoid unnecessary disturbance of the Latin faithful.

See *Chrismation with Holy Myron/Confirmation; Eucharistic Communion of Children.*

Spiritual Relationship

The Eastern code, unlike the Latin one, maintains the impediment of spiritual relationship. "From baptism there arises a spiritual relationship between a sponsor and the baptized person and the parents of the same that invalidates marriage. If a baptism is repeated under condition, a spiritual relationship does not arise, unless the same sponsor was employed for the second ceremony" (CCEO c. 811). Therefore, a marriage between the sponsor and either the baptized or his or her parents cannot be celebrated validly. Although this impediment has been repealed in the Latin code, the Latin sponsor who wishes to marry the Eastern baptized or his or her parent could not do so validly because the Eastern baptized or his or her parent would be bound by the Eastern code. To do so validly, the Eastern party must request a dispensation from the competent local hierarch (CCEO c. 795, §1; CIC c. 1078, §1).

Sponsor at Baptism

In establishing the requirements to fulfill the role of a sponsor at baptism, the Eastern code distinguishes between necessary requirements for validity and those for liceity. The Latin code, instead, deals with the requirements for liceity only. In the Eastern Churches, from baptism there arises a spiritual relationship between a sponsor and the baptized person and the parents of the same that invalidates marriage (CCEO c. 811).

Required Age
Both codes prescribe this requirement for liceity only. According to the Eastern code, the required age of sponsors is determined by the particular law of each Church *sui iuris*, while the Latin code requires that a person must have completed the sixteenth year of age (CCEO c. 685, §2; CIC c. 874, §1, 2°).

Reception of the Sacraments of Initiation

Both codes require that the sponsors be initiated with all three sacraments of baptism, chrismation and the Eucharist (CCEO c. 685, §1, 1°; CIC c. 874, §1, 3°). For the Eastern Churches this condition is *ad validitatem.* The sponsor should in fact assist the parents in the Christian education of the child, while in the case of an adult baptism the sponsor is to assist in the preparatory phase of the Christian initiation and to help the newly baptized person lead a Christian life in harmony with baptism and fulfill faithfully the obligations connected with it (CCEO c. 684, §2; CIC c. 872). Note that in the Eastern Churches, as a rule, the three sacraments of baptism, chrismation and the Eucharist are administered at the same time (CCEO cc. 694-695). In the Latin Church, instead, these sacraments are administered separately, unless one is dealing with an adult. The conference of bishops can determine for the sacrament of confirmation another age besides that of discretion (CIC c. 891).

Member of the Catholic Church

For a person to fulfill validly the role of a sponsor it is necessary that he or she belongs to the Catholic Church, but, for a just cause, a Christian of another Eastern non-Catholic Church may be admitted, always along with a Catholic sponsor (CCEO c 685, §1, 2°; §3).

The Latin code states: "§1. 3° To be permitted to take on the function of sponsor a person must be a Catholic who has been confirmed and has already received the most holy sacrament of the Eucharist and who leads a life of faith in keeping with the function to be taken on. §2. A baptized person who belongs to a non-Catholic ecclesial community is not to participate except together with a Catholic sponsor and then only as a witness (*ut testis*) of the baptism. (CIC c. 874, §1, 3°; §2).

The Ecumenical Directory (n. 98), revisiting these norms, upholds the Catholic principle that sponsors, in a liturgical and canonical sense, should themselves be members of the Church or Ecclesial Community in which the baptism is being celebrated. They do not merely undertake a responsibility for the Christian education of the person being baptized as a relation or friend; they are also there as representatives of a community of faith, standing as guarantees of the candidate's faith and desire for ecclesial communion.

Based on common baptism, however, and because of ties of blood or friendship, a baptized person who belongs to another Ecclesial Community may be admitted as a witness to the baptism, but only together with a Catholic sponsor. A Catholic may do the same for a person being baptized in another Ecclesial Community.

Because of the close communion between the Catholic Church and the Eastern Orthodox Churches, it is permissible for a just cause for an Eastern Orthodox to act as a sponsor; together with a Catholic sponsor, at the baptism of a Catholic infant or adult, so long as there is provision for the Catholic education of the person being baptized and it is clear that the sponsor is a suitable one.

A Catholic is not forbidden to serve as a sponsor in an Eastern Orthodox Church, if he or she is invited to do so. In this case, the duty of providing for the Christian education binds primarily the sponsor who belongs to the Church in which the child or adult is baptized.

Other concomitant features are listed in c. 685 of the Eastern code and in c. 874 of the Latin code, with the only difference being that for the Eastern Churches they are *ad validitatem*.

Transfer to Another Church *Sui Iuris*

The transfer of a Catholic's membership to an Eastern Church *sui iuris* or to the Latin Church, commonly called "change of rite," can validly take place according to the canonical norms and with the consent of the Holy See. Obviously, such consent can be justified only in exceptional circumstances, with due documentation, and after having heard the two concerned bishops, *a quo et ad quem* (CCEO c. 32). The Latin code similarly states that, after the reception of baptism, a person is enrolled in another Church *sui iuris* after having obtained permission (*licentiam*) from the Apostolic See (CIC c. 112, §1).

Canon 32, §2 presumes this consent of the Holy See (*consensus praesumitur*) for the transfer of a Catholic of an eparchy of one Church *sui iuris* to another Church *sui iuris* which has its own eparchy in the same territory. Since the Latin code does not have such a presumption, a General Rescript of the Secretary of State in 1992 extended it to the Christian faithful of the Latin Church (AAS 85 [1993] 81).

Thus, if a Latin Catholic asks to transfer to an Eastern Church *sui iuris* that has an eparchy in the same territory, the consent of the Holy See is presumed, provided that the two concerned bishops are in agreement. For instance, in Pittsburgh there are a Byzantine archeparch for the Ruthenian faithful and a Latin bishop for the Latin faithful: if a Latin asks to transfer to the Ruthenian Church, the mutual approval of the Byzantine archeparch and the Latin bishop suffices.

It should be noted here that, since the 1992 General Rescript of the Secretary of State, various decisions of the Congregation for the Eastern Churches have excluded the cases of Eastern faithful asking for a transfer to the Latin Church whose diocese is in the same territory, even though the two bishops are in agreement. This restrictive application seems to be justified by the distinctive ecclesiological and canonical concept of a Church *sui iuris,* as well as by the appropriate concept of *ritus*, understood as a liturgical, theological, spiritual and disciplinary heritage. In the unity of the universal Church, every Catholic is to maintain, honor and observe the rite of his or her own Church *sui iuris*. Nevertheless, the Holy See as supreme arbiter of relations among Churches and for the good of souls provides in particular cases for those persons, communities or regions that ask for such transfers.

In the Eastern regions the Congregation for the Eastern Churches rarely authorizes the transfer from an Eastern Church *sui iuris* to another, and even more reluctantly to the Latin Church. Authorization for a transfer is more frequently given in the so-called diaspora when, among other reasons, members of the same family belong to different Churches.

MATRIMONIAL ISSUES

Annulment of Marriages of Non-Catholics

An annulment is the declaration by judicial sentence of the invalidity of a marriage from the beginning of its celebration (matrimonium in fieri). Divorce is the dissolution of a marriage validly celebrated (matrimonium in facto esse). It is generally accepted today that non-Catholics, baptized or not, who, after having obtained a divorce, desire to enter marriage with a Catholic party may seek an ecclesiastical annulment of the previous marriage (CCEO c. 1134; CIC c. 1476).

See *Marriages of Catholics with Divorced Orthodox and Protestant; Orthodox Sentences of Divorce.*

Canonical Form and Inter-ritual Marriages

Eastern and Latin Norms

The Eastern Churches hold that "only those marriages are valid that are celebrated with a sacred rite, in the presence of the local hierarch, local pastor, or a priest who has been given the faculty of blessing the marriage by either of them, and at least two witnesses" (CCEO c. 828 §1). The same canon §2 also states that the "very intervention of a priest (bishop or presbyter) who assists and blesses is regarded as a sacred rite for the present purpose." It is self-evident that the liturgical form and the juridical form of marriage in the Eastern Churches are entirely concurrent. The subjects of this form, including Eastern Catholics who have publicly abandoned the Catholic faith and joined a non-Catholic Church or community, are bound by the Catholic norms for the celebration of marriage (CCEO c. 834, §1).

The Latin code, on the other hand, establishes that "only those marriages are valid which are contracted before the local ordinary, pastor, or a priest or deacon delegated by either of them, who assist, and before two witnesses" (CIC c. 1108 §1). Canon 1112 of the same code prescribes that "where there is a lack of priests and deacons, the diocesan bishop can delegate lay persons to assist at marriages." The person who "assists at a marriage" is understood to be one who is present, asks for the manifestation of the consent of the contracting parties, and receives it in the name of the Church (CIC c. 1108 §2). This form must be observed if at least one of the parties contracting marriage was baptized in the Catholic Church or received into it and has not defected from it by a formal act (CIC c. 1117). Consequently, a Latin Catholic who has posited a formal act of abandoning the Catholic faith and has joined a non-Catholic Church or community is not liable to observe the Catholic canonical form.

Difference of Inter-ritual Norms

- The marriage of Eastern parties whether they are subjects or non-subjects, provided that at least one of the parties is ascribed in the Church *sui iuris* of the celebrating local pastor, is validly blessed; for liceity the marriage is to be celebrated before the pastor of the groom (CCEO cc. 829, §1; 831, §2).
- The discipline of the Eastern Churches does not allow deacons or lay persons to celebrate/bless marriages (CCEO cc. 828, 830). The marriages of Eastern Catholics celebrated before a delegated deacon or lay person are invalid.
- The marriage between an Eastern and a Latin can validly be celebrated by the local pastor provided that one of them is his subject (CCEO c. 829; CIC c. 1109).
- The marriage between an Eastern and a Latin cannot validly be celebrated before a deacon, whether Eastern or Latin. Some canon lawyers hold the contrary opinion in theory, that is, that the marriage between an Eastern and a Latin could be validly celebrated in a Latin parish before a duly delegated Latin deacon. Despite this canonical opinion, local Latin ordinaries or pastors should not delegate a deacon to assist at such marriages. In the judicial forum such a marriage, involving at least one Eastern faithful, Catholic or Orthodox, would be declared null on the grounds of lack of the *sacer ritus.*

Delegation for Marriages

Eastern Catholics often ask for permission to celebrate their marriage according to the liturgical rite of the Latin Church with a Latin priest as officiant; the same happens with Latin Catholics who want their weddings celebrated in the liturgical rite of an Eastern Church. Eastern bishops of the place and local pastors can give the faculty to bless a determined marriage within their own territorial boundaries to priests of any Church *sui iuris*, including the Latin Church (CCEO c. 830 §1). Similarly, the Latin local ordinaries and pastors can delegate Eastern priests to assist and bless the marriages of Latin Catholics within the limits of their territory (CIC c. 1111, §1).

One must keep in mind, however, that, except when the hierarch or the pastor are of another Church *sui iuris,* the celebration must follow *ad liceitatem* the liturgical rite of the spouses, or of one of them in an inter-ritual marriage (CCEO c. 40, §3). Although a celebration according to another rite is illicit, it can be permitted in a specific case by the Holy See (LI 83). The general norm established by both codes requires that the sacred minister celebrate the sacraments in his own rite, but the law itself provides an exception in the case of marriage (CCEO c. 674, §2; CIC c. 846, §2).

Thus, a duly delegated Eastern priest may celebrate the marriage of Latin faithful according to the Latin rite; to officiate at their wedding according to an Eastern rite requires the specific faculty from the Holy See. A duly delegated

Latin priest may celebrate the marriage of Eastern faithful according to the Eastern rite; to officiate at their wedding according to the Latin rite requires the specific faculty from the Holy See. However, a Latin priest who serves as the proper pastor of Eastern faithful can licitly celebrate the marriage of said Christians in the Latin rite (CCEO c. 916, §4).

Dispensation from Canonical Form for an Eastern Catholic to Marry a Protestant or Non-baptized

An Eastern Catholic may celebrate marriage with a non-baptized person with a dispensation from the impediment of disparity of worship (CCEO cc. 803, 795); he or she may marry a baptized Protestant with the prior permission of the competent authority (CCEO c. 813). As regards the canonical form, the marriages of Eastern Catholics are valid only if they are celebrated with a sacred rite in the presence of the local hierarch or pastor, or a priest delegated by either of them, and at least of two witnesses.

By the phrase *sacred rite* is understood the intervention of a priest (bishop or presbyter) who assists in the name of the Church at the exchange of consent, and liturgically blesses the marriage (CCEO c. 828). This canonical form is to be followed for validity (CCEO c. 834, §1). Dispensing from the canonical form is reserved to the Holy See or the patriarch within the patriarchal territory (CCEO c. 835).

The Latin code, on the other hand, gives the right of dispensing from the form in individual cases to the ordinary of the place (CIC c. 1127, §2). Such a dispensation implies the possibility of being married in a public wedding ceremony before a Protestant pastor, an officiant of a non-Christian faith or even a civil official. Consequently, in the case of an Eastern Catholic subject to a Latin ordinary (CCEO c. 916, §5), the local ordinary cannot validly grant a canonical form dispensation. Of course, the Holy See can delegate this faculty to the Apostolic Nuncio of that area.

See *Marriages of Eastern faithful and Non-baptized in Latin Territories; Mixed Marriages.*

Dispensation from Impediments in Inter-ritual Marriages

In marriages between Catholics, Eastern and Latin, an impediment, even if only one of the parties has it, renders the marriage invalid (CCEO c. 790, §2).

The local Eastern hierarch has the right to dispense from ecclesiastical impediments the Christian faithful subject to him wherever they may be at the time are as well as other Christian faithful ascribed to another Church *sui iuris* who are actually present within the territorial boundaries of his eparchy.

The hierarch is not authorized to dispense from the following impediments: sacred orders; public perpetual vow of chastity in a religious institute, unless it is an institute of eparchial right; conjugicide. Dispensation from these impediments is reserved to the Holy See. Nonetheless, a patriarch can dispense from the impediments of conjugicide and public perpetual vow of chastity in any religious institute within his patriarchal territory. A dispensation is never granted from the impediment of consanguinity in the direct line or in the second degree of the collateral line (CCEO c. 795).

The local Latin ordinary can dispense his own subjects residing anywhere and all Catholics actually present in his territory (including Eastern faithful entrusted to his pastoral care) from all impediments of ecclesiastical law except those whose dispensation is reserved to the Holy See. The reserved impediments are: sacred orders, a public perpetual vow of chastity in a religious institute of pontifical right; the crime of conjugicide. Dispensation from the impediment of consanguinity in the direct line or in the second degree of the collateral line is never granted (CIC c. 1078).

Inter-eparchial and Inter-ritual Tribunals

The eparchial bishops of various Churches *sui iuris*, including those of the Latin Church, who exercising governance within the same area, can agree among themselves to establish a common tribunal, to adjudicate both contentious and penal cases of the Christian faithful subject to any one of these eparchial bishops. If suitable judges and other tribunal officers are not readily available, eparchial bishops should see to the establishment of a common tribunal. The eparchial bishops who agree to a common tribunal must designate from among themselves one who will have the power over the tribunal that an eparchial bishop has regarding his own tribunal. Appeals from the sentences of a common tribunal of first instance are made to a tribunal designated to this function in a stable manner by the Apostolic Signatura (CCEO c. 1068; CIC c. 1423).

See *Matrimonial Judicial Causes.*

Marriages by Proxy

For the valid celebration of marriage the Eastern code requires the parties to be present together (*partes sint praesentes una simul*) and mutually express their marriage consent. Marriage cannot be validly celebrated by proxy unless the particular law of the respective Church *sui iuris* states otherwise, in which case, it must set forth the conditions under which such a marriage can be celebrated (CCEO c. 837).

The Eastern norm differs from the Latin one (CIC c. 1105): The theology and polity of the Eastern Churches does not fully accept the juridical institute of a proxy marriage; the Latin Church, on the other hand, supports such a juridical institute because of the mobility of people and the political-social circumstances of our days. By common law, the Eastern Catholic Churches do not allow marriages by proxy; but the norm adds the clause "unless the particular law of the respective Church *sui iuris* establishes otherwise," giving legislative authority to each Church *sui iuris* rather than to the individual hierarch. If the particular law of a Church *sui iuris* should authorize marriages by proxy, it must lay out the conditions under which such marriages can be celebrated. These conditions would be those described by the Latin code:

1. To celebrate a marriage validly by proxy it is required that: a) there is a special mandate to enter into marriage with a specific person; b) the proxy is designated by the one mandating and fulfills this function personally.
2. To be valid the mandate must be signed by the one mandating and by the parish priest or ordinary of the place where the mandate is given, or by a priest delegated by either of them, or at least by two witnesses, or it must be made by means of a document which is authentic according to the norm of civil law.
3. If the one mandating cannot write, this is to be noted in the mandate itself and another witness is to be added who also signs the document; otherwise, the mandate is invalid.
4. If the one mandating revokes the mandate or develops amentia before the proxy enters into marriage on his or her behalf, the marriage is invalid even if the proxy or the other spouse does not know this (CIC c. 1105).

Marriages of Catholics with Divorced Orthodox or Protestants

Doctrinal and Canonical Principle

The Catholic Church recognizes the marriage of Orthodox Christians celebrated with a sacred rite, that is, with the intervention of a priest who assists and blesses.

As for Protestant faithful, the Catholic Church acknowledges whatever form is prescribed or allowed by the proper law of the Ecclesial Community to which the parties were subject at the time of the celebration of marriage, provided that marital consent has been expressed in a public manner (CCEO cc. 780, 781, 828; DC art. 2).

Still, the Catholic Church, the Orthodox Church and the Protestant communities greatly differ in matrimonial matters. Catholic doctrine holds that a marriage validly celebrated and consummated is indissoluble by divine law, while other Churches and Ecclesial Communities accept in doctrine and praxis the possibility of various reasons for its dissolution. This difference has juridical and pastoral consequences for a mixed marriage: A Catholic cannot validly marry a baptized or unbaptized divorced person who is bound by a prior marriage (CIC c. 1085; CCEO c. 802).

Anticipated Cases

- An Orthodox party, after having obtained a divorce from his or her legitimately-celebrated Church marriage, intends to enter into a new marriage with a free Catholic party. In some countries, this act of divorce is nothing other than a "declaration of nullity" issued by the

Orthodox bishop that ratifies the judicial sentence of divorce of the civil court. With this ecclesiastical ratification, the Orthodox party is permitted to enter a new religious marriage. The Catholic Church does not recognize any divorce decree of a legitimately celebrated marriage issued by any civil or religious authority whatsoever. Marriage, in the order of creation and in the sacramental order, is indissoluble by divine law, natural law and positive law. A marriage between a divorced Orthodox party and a Catholic party cannot validly be celebrated because of the impediment of the previous marriage bond on the part of the Orthodox – *ob impedimentum prioris matrimonii* (CIC c. 1085, §1; CCEO c. 802, §1).

- A Protestant party, after having obtained a divorce from his or her legitimately celebrated marriage according to the law of his or her Ecclesial Community intends to enter a new marriage with a free Catholic party. In this case too the Catholic Church does not recognize any divorce decree of a legitimately celebrated marriage issued by any civil or religious authority whatsoever, for marriage is indissoluble by divine law, natural law and positive law. A marriage between a divorced Protestant party and a Catholic party cannot validly be celebrated because of the impediment of the previous marriage bond on the part of the Protestant.

- Two Orthodox faithful, after having married only civilly, obtain a divorce. One of them intends to marry a free Catholic. This marriage can be celebrated in the Catholic Church because the validity of a marriage between Orthodox requires celebration before an Orthodox priest. Consequently, the marriage of the divorced Orthodox was invalid because of a defective form from both the Orthodox and the Catholic standpoint.

See *Mixed Marriages; Orthodox Sentences of Divorce.*

Marriages of Eastern Faithful and Non-Baptized in Latin Territory

A marriage between two persons, one of whom has been baptized in the Catholic Church (Latin or Eastern) and the other not baptized at all, cannot validly be celebrated without a dispensation granted by the competent ecclesiastical authority (CCEO c.803; CIC c.1086). This impediment of ecclesiastical law is called "disparity of worship." The councils of Chalcedon (c. 14) and in Trullo (c. 72) declared absolutely null and void the marriage between a Christian and a non-baptized person. Today's Orthodox Churches still do not recognize such marriages, even though some among them support flexibility (*oikonomia*) in the matter.

The Catholic Church, recognizing the inalienable natural right of a person to marry, grants a dispensation from this impediment for a just and reasonable cause if certain conditions are fulfilled. Specifically, the Catholic party is to declare that he or she is prepared to remove all dangers of defecting from the faith and is to make a sincere promise to do all in his or her power to see that their children are baptized and brought up in the Catholic Church. The other party is to be informed at an appropriate time about the Catholic's promises in such a way that it is certain that he or she is truly aware of the promise and obligation of the Catholic party.

In territories where there is a proper hierarch of a Church *sui iuris* to which the Eastern party belongs, that hierarch is competent to grant the dispensation from the impediment of disparity of worship. The form prescribed for the valid celebration of marriage, however, must include a sacred rite in the presence of the local hierarch, local pastor, or a priest (Eastern or Latin) who possesses the faculty of blessing the marriage of one of them, and at least two witnesses (CCEO c. 828).

In territories where there is no proper hierarch of the Church *sui iuris* to which the Eastern party belongs, the competent authority to grant the dispensation is the local ordinary of another Church *sui iuris*, including the Latin Church, depending on the domicile or quasi-domicile of the Eastern party. The form for the valid celebration of marriage is that prescribed in the above mentioned canon. Dispensation from the form for the celebration of marriage prescribed by law is reserved to the Holy See (CCEO c. 835).

See *Delegation for Marriages; Dispensation from Impediments in Inter-ritual Marriages.*

Marriage of Eastern Faithful Who Has Publicly Rejected the Catholic Faith

The Eastern priest, beyond the cases defined by law, is not to bless, without the permission (*licentia*) of the local hierarch, the marriage of a person who has publicly rejected the Catholic faith, even if that person did not become a member of a non-Catholic Church or Ecclesial Community (CCEO c. 789). Furthermore, a Catholic who has notoriously rejected the Catholic faith and transferred to a non-Catholic Church or Ecclesial Community is still bound by Catholic law. "The form for the celebration of marriage by law is to be observed if at least one of the parties celebrating the marriage was baptized in the Catholic Church or was received into it (*in ecclesia catholica baptizata vel in eandem recepta est*)" (CCEO c. 834, §1). A baptized Catholic, even if he or she commits apostasy, heresy or schism is always bound by the law of the Catholic Church.

The celebration of this marriage without the permission of the local hierarch is forbidden because the celebrating party has incurred a censure, but, even if the person is not under censure, public rejection of the Catholic faith precludes the celebration. The permission the local hierarch requires the formalities of CCOE c. 814 on mixed marriages: For a just cause the local hierarch can grant permission ... (when) the following conditions are fulfilled: "1° the Catholic party declares that he or she is prepared to remove dangers of falling away (*pericula a fide deficiendi removere*) from the faith and makes a sincere promise to do all in his or her power to have all the children baptized and educated in the Catholic Church; [...] 3° both parties are to be instructed on the essential ends and properties (*de finibus et proprietatibus*) of marriage, which are not to be excluded by either spouse." These norms apply as well for marriages between Catholics and non-practicing or atheistic persons.

A Latin diocesan bishop is not to grant permission for the marriage of a person who has notoriously rejected the Catholic faith (*notorie catholicam fidem abiecerit*) unless the norms on mixed marriages (CIC c. 1125) have been observed with necessary adaptation. Indeed, the Latin code states that the canonical form of marriage must be observed by the Catholic party, provided that he or she has not abandoned the Catholic Church by a formal act (CIC c. 117). A Latin Catholic who has posited a formal act of publicly rejecting the Catholic faith (and possibly transferring to a non-Catholic Church or Ecclesial Community) is not subject to Catholic law.

Therefore, when Eastern Catholics are subject to a Latin bishop, he should not permit their marriages if they have publicly abandoned the Catholic faith unless the necessary canonical conditions have been fulfilled (CIC c. 1125).

Marriages of Eastern Minors Against Their Parents' Will

The Eastern code sets the age for the valid celebration of marriage at sixteen years for a man and fourteen for a woman (CCEO c. 800, §1). Nonetheless, without the permission of the local hierarch, a priest is not to bless the marriage of minors without their parents' knowledge. According to canon 909, §1, "A person who has completed the eighteenth year of age has reached majority; below this age, a person is a minor."

The Latin code states that a duly qualified witness "is not to assist without the permission of the local ordinary at a marriage of a minor person when the parents are unaware or reasonably opposed" (CIC c. 1071). The reason for this cautionary measure is not to protect marriage so much as the institution of the family; more precisely. it is the value of the parent-child relationship that is being safeguarded.

Thus, when Eastern parents, subject to a Latin pastor, are unaware or reasonably opposed to their minor child's marriage, the celebration of the marriage should not take place without the permission of the local diocesan bishop.

Marriage Law

Inter-ritual Marriages

Both codes assert that the marriages of Catholics are governed not only by divine law but also by canon law (CCEO c. 780, §1; CIC c. 1059). Marriage between a Latin Catholic and an Eastern Catholic is governed, with due regard to divine law, by the canons of the two respective Churches *sui iuris*. In substantive matrimonial law, however, there are certain differences, particularly in regard to impediments and canonical form.

Moreover, regarding impediments in general, the Eastern code states that "diriment impediments are not to be established by the particular law of a Church *sui iuris* except for a most grave cause, after having consulted with the eparchial bishops of other Churches *sui iuris* who have an interest, and after consultation with the Holy See" (c.792). The Latin code explicitly prescribes: "Only the supreme authority of the Church has the right to establish other impediments for the baptized" (c.1075, §2). When, therefore, an Eastern Church *sui iuris* establishes additional impediments, these also affect marriage between a Latin and an Eastern Catholic on the principle that "An impediment, even if only one of the parties has it, still renders the marriage invalid" (CCEO c. 790, §2).

Impediments in the Two Codes

In the area of matrimonial impediments, the two codes display certain differences, specifically with regards to the impediments of affinity, public propriety and spiritual relationship:

"Affinity invalidates a marriage in the direct line in any degree whatsoever; in the collateral line, in the second degree (CCEO c. 809, §1), while the Latin code limits affinity solely to "the direct line in any degree" (c. 1092). According to Eastern law, a marriage between a man and his deceased wife's sister is invalid, and vice versa. Thus, although a Latin widower is free to marry his Latin sister-in-law, he cannot validly marry his Eastern sister-in-law insofar as she is bound by the impediment in the Eastern code. The Eastern party needs a dispensation from this impediment, which can be granted by the hierarch of the place of the same Church *sui iuris.*

According to CCEO c. 810, §1, "the impediment of public propriety arises: 1° from an invalid marriage after which the couple has lived together; 2° from notorious or public concubinage; 3° from the cohabitation of a couple who are bound to the form of marriage celebration prescribed by law but have attempted marriage before a civil official or a non-Catholic minister. §2. This impediment invalidates marriage in the first degree of the direct line between a man and the blood relatives of the woman and between a woman and the blood relatives of the man." This impediment is by ecclesiastical law and is perpetual by its nature, unless a dispensation is granted by the local diocesan/eparchial bishop.

The Latin norm, instead, says that "the impediment of public propriety arises from an invalid marriage after the establishment of common life or from notorious or public concubinage. It nullifies marriage in the first degree of the direct line between the man and the blood relatives of the woman, and vice versa" (CIC c.1093), and this because a civil marriage has always been considered non-existent (*Communicationes* 15 [1983] 224).

The Eastern code retains the impediment of spiritual relationship arising from baptism. "From baptism there arises a spiritual relationship between a sponsor and the baptized person and the parents of the same that invalidates marriage" (CCEO c. 811, §1). This impediment has been abrogated in the Latin code. Nonetheless, although a Latin Catholic is not bound by the impediment if he or she marries someone who is not a Catholic of an Eastern Church, he or she is effectively bound by it if the other party is an Eastern Catholic insofar as the impediment affecting the other party would invalidate his or her marriage. The dispensation for Eastern parties who are bound by the impediment of spiritual relationship can be granted by the hierarch of the place of the same Church *sui iuris*.

Matrimonial Consent in the Two Codes

The Latin code in c. 1102, §2 states that "Marriage entered into under a condition concerning the past or the present, is valid or not, as the condition is fulfilled or not." The Eastern code, however, in c. 826 states: "Marriage based on a condition cannot be validly celebrated." The difference in these rules, therefore, raises a question of validity of a marriage between a Latin party who places a condition and an Eastern party who does not. Even though the Eastern party has not violated the law, their marriage would be invalid, because a marriage cannot be valid for one party and invalid for the other; consent is the only act that must be valid for both parties. The opposite opinion, however, favoring validity in just such a case, has found some support. The Orthodox Churches do not accept a marriage celebrated under a condition precisely because of the "*ritus sacer*" required for the validity of the sacrament. The sacrament of marriage cannot be celebrated under any condition whatsoever.

Differences in Canonical Form

The Eastern code states: "Only those marriages are valid that are celebrated with a sacred rite, in the presence of the local hierarch, local pastor, or a priest who has been given the faculty of blessing the marriage by either of them, and at least two witnesses" (c. 828, §1). The second paragraph of the same canon clarifies the meaning of "sacred rite" by adding: "The very intervention of a priest who assists and blesses is regarded as a sacred rite for the present purpose."

The Latin code, instead, states: "Only those marriages are valid which are contracted in the presence of the local ordinary, or of the pastor, or of a priest or a deacon delegated by either of them, who must assist, and in the presence of two witnesses" (c. 1108). Furthermore, c. 1112, §1 adds: "Where there is a lack of priests and deacons, the diocesan bishop can delegate lay persons to assist at marriages." Canon 1108, §2 explains the meaning of 'assist': "Only the person who, being present, requests the manifestation of the consent of the contracting parties and receives it in the name of the Church is understood to assist at the marriage." All the Eastern Churches – Orthodox and Catholic – maintain that the liturgical and juridical form of marriage occur simultaneously and are inseparable.

Latin Tribunals and Eastern Marriages

The ongoing migration of Eastern Catholics to the so-called *regiones occidentales* has brought about new situations for those who often find themselves in a territory under the jurisdiction of a Latin ordinary (CCEO c.

916, §5), where there is no hierarchy of their own nor necessary offices, like, e.g., their own tribunals.

The 2005 Instruction of the Pontifical Council for the Interpretation of Legislative Texts, *Dignitas Connubii* (art. 16) tackles this problem: " A tribunal of the Latin Church, ... can hear the cause of the nullity of the marriage of Catholics of another Church *sui iuris*: 1° *ipso iure*, in a territory where, besides the local ordinary of the Latin Church, there is no other local hierarch of any other Church *sui iuris*, or where the pastoral care of the faithful of the Church *sui iuris* in question has been entrusted to the local ordinary of the Latin Church by designation of the Holy See or at least with its assent (CCEO c. 916, §5); 2° in other cases by reason of an extension of competence granted by the Apostolic Signatura whether stably or *ad casum*. In such case, the tribunal of the Latin Church must proceed according to its own procedural law, but the question of the nullity of marriage is to be decided according to the laws of the Church *sui iuris* to which the parties belong."

This norm regulates the competent forum for the causes of nullity of marriages of these Eastern Catholics heard by Latin tribunals. The Latin tribunal on their part are required to proceed according to the substantive norms of the Church *sui iuris* of the parties.

See *Matrimonial Judicial Causes; Dispensation from Impediments in Inter-Ritual Marriages; Canonical Form and Inter-ritual Marriages; Mixed Marriages; Marriages of Catholics with Divorced Orthodox and Protestants; Marriages of Eastern Minors Against their Parents Will; Marriages of Eastern Faithful who Publicly Rejected the Catholic Faith; Marriages of Eastern Faithful and Non-baptized in Latin Territories.*

Matrimonial Judicial Causes

The phenomenon of human mobility in general and the constant migration of Eastern Christian faithful to territories of the Latin Church in particular have been growing in the last few decades. Consequently, these Eastern faithful find themselves in a Latin milieu and under the jurisdiction of Latin ordinaries (CCEO c. 916, §5). A particular aspect of this situation regards the matrimonial judicial causes of Eastern Catholics introduced in Latin tribunals.

Eastern Catholics and Latin Tribunals

The Pontifical Council for the Interpretation of Legislative Texts, with the approval of the supreme legislator, published on January 25, 2005, the instruction *Dignitas Connubii* to be observed by diocesan and inter-diocesan tribunals in handling causes of nullity of marriage. Article 16 of this instruction refers to the competence for causes involving Eastern Catholics:

"§1. A tribunal of the Latin Church can hear the cause of the nullity of the marriage of Catholics of another Church *sui iuris*: *ipso iure* in a territory where, besides the local ordinary of the Latin Church, there is no other local hierarch of any other Church *sui iuris*, or when the pastoral care of the faithful of the Church *sui iuris* in question has been entrusted to the local ordinary of the Latin Church; in other cases by reason of an extension of competence granted by the Apostolic Signatura whether stably or *ad casum*.

"§2. In such case, the tribunal of the Latin Church must proceed according to its own procedural law, but the question of the nullity of marriage is to be decided according to the laws of the Church *sui iuris* to which the parties belong."

It is well known that there are differences in substantive matrimonial law between the Eastern code and the Latin code, particularly in the matter of matrimonial impediments, canonical form, and dispensations. Therefore, in examining the causes of matrimonial nullity of Eastern Catholics, the Latin judge, besides following the procedural norms of his own Church, has to apply the laws of the Church *sui iuris* to which the parties belong.

See *Marriage Law; Marriage of Catholics with Divorced Orthodox and Protestants.*

Orthodox Sentences of Divorce

Principle

The Catholic Church recognizes declarations of matrimonial nullity issued by the Orthodox Churches according to their own norms, even if these do not exist in Catholic canonical procedure – provided they are not contrary to divine law. Catholic teaching, however, does not recognize a divorce by reason of adultery or any other cause, as occurs in some Orthodox Churches, nor the application of the principle of *oikonomia*, because such dissolutions suppose the intervention of ecclesiastical authority in dissolving the matrimonial bond of a valid sacrament. The Catholic Church does not recognize any sentence of divorce of a legitimate Catholic or non-Catholic marriage. The same applies to Protestant marriages legitimately celebrated according to the law of their Ecclesial Communities.

Because the kind of dissolution granted by sentence in Orthodox Churches is difficult to understand, certain doubts arise. In their sentences or decisions, the distinction between "declaration of nullity" and "divorce" is missing, and the justifying grounds are also lacking. In a case of doubt, one must presume the marriage valid until the contrary is proven, because marriage enjoys the favor of the law. Therefore, when in need of greater clarification, it is more acceptable *ad cautelam* to follow the current praxis of assessing the validity of Orthodox marriages according to the norms of Catholic procedures before allowing a new marriage between a Catholic and a divorced Orthodox.

When it is not a matter of marriage nullity but of *oikonomia* and dissolution, one must conclude that, at least until demonstrated otherwise, the validity of the marriage must stand. The marriage of Orthodox faithful celebrated in the Orthodox Church is valid and enjoys the favor of the law until the contrary is proven. Since the first marriage enjoys the favor of the law, the impediment of *ligamen* (existing bond) is presumed present, preventing the Orthodox spouse from entering a new marriage with a Catholic until the good offices of a competent Catholic tribunal decides otherwise.

Non-Catholic Faithful and Catholic Tribunals

In the current state of affairs, an Orthodox or Protestant Christian planning to celebrate a marriage with a Catholic party can bring his or her case to a Catholic tribunal for adjudication. "Anyone, either baptized or non-baptized, can bring an action in a trial. However, a party who is legitimately summoned must respond" (CCEO c.1134; CIC c.1476).

The ministry of the Catholic judge, upon request of the divorced non-Catholic party, is legitimately and pastorally justified by the right of the Catholic party to enter marriage with this non-Catholic person and the fact that the non-Catholic's divorced status interferes with that right, preventing a new marriage. A competent Catholic tribunal, Latin or Eastern, must proceed according to canonical matrimonial process (CIC c. 1673; CCEO c. 1359) and the instruction *Dignitas Connubii,* art. 4, on the law governing non-Catholic marriages.

Criteria for the Catholic Judge

When the ecclesiastical judge is called to render a sentence or decision on a case of matrimonial nullity of baptized non-Catholic persons, he should take cognizance of the following:

- Apart from divine law, the law to be applied is that to which the parties were subject at the time of the celebration of marriage;
- As for the form of celebration of marriage, the Catholic Church recognizes any form prescribed by the Church or Ecclesial Community the parties belonged to at the time of the celebration, provided that consent was expressed publicly, and, if one party was Orthodox, that the sacred rite or blessing was imparted.
- The sacred rite, that is, the sacramental blessing by the priest is for the Orthodox a constitutive element for the valid celebration of marriage. When it is lacking, ascertaining the freedom of the Orthodox party does not require a judicial procedure; the administrative process suffices. The Pontifical Council for the Interpretation of Legislative Texts, on June 26, 1984, declared that Orthodox who, though bound by canonical form, entered a civil marriage, are not required to follow the documentary process (CIC c. 1686; CCEO c. 1372): the pre-nuptial investigation by the pastor is sufficient (CIC cc. 1066-1067; CCEO c. 785). In other words, the pastor, in establishing that nothing stands in the way of the valid and licit celebration of the marriage, makes note of the fact (*AAS* 77 [1984] 746-747; *Communicationes* 77 [1995] n. 2, 208-209). Orthodox who entered a civil marriage and then divorced, are free to celebrate marriage with a Catholic party.
- With respect to the marriages of Protestants, the ecclesiastical tribunals must judge their validity with regard to the form of the celebration.

Catholic law recognizes any form prescribed or admitted by the law to which the Protestants were subject at the time of the celebration of the marriage, provided that the consent was expressed in a public form. With the present codes, Protestants are completely free of the marriage law of the Catholic Church. However, they are bound by civil law because their own Ecclesial Communities have declared marriage to be a secular affair subject to the State.

See *Marriage of Catholics with Divorced Orthodox and Protestants; Annulment of Marriages of Non-Catholics.*

ORDINATION

Celibacy and Married State of Eastern Clerics

Principle

The Eastern and the Latin Churches follow a different discipline on the celibacy of their clergy. The Eastern code, in accordance with the decree *Presbyterorum Ordinis* of Vatican II (PO 16), emphasizes celibacy as well as the married state of clerics: "Clerical celibacy chosen for the sake of the kingdom of heaven and highly suited to the priesthood is to be greatly esteemed everywhere, according to the tradition of the entire Church; likewise, the state of married clerics, sanctioned in the practice of primitive Church and in the Eastern Churches through the ages, is to be held in honor" (c. 373). This canon underlines the convenience and great esteem the Eastern Churches always had towards the celibate and married clergy in accord with the tradition of the universal Church and the respect of the Eastern Churches *sui iuris*.

A widowed Eastern priest or deacon, however, is not permitted to celebrate a new marriage. This is an impediment of ecclesiastical law that only the Holy See may dispense (CCEO c. 795). It is an ancient norm of the entire Church established by the Apostolic Canons (c. 26) of the first ecumenical councils and reconfirmed by the sixth canon of the Council in Trullo (691-692): "Whereas it is stated in the apostolic canons that 'from among the celibate men promoted to the clergy, only the readers and cantors may marry,' so do we, observing this, decree that henceforth no deacon nor presbyter, should in any wise be at liberty to arrange for himself a matrimonial union after his ordination; if he dares to do this, he shall be deposed."

Present Norm

The Eastern code states that "the particular law of each Church *sui iuris* or special norms established by the Holy See are to be followed in admitting married men to sacred orders" (c. 758 §3). This means that each Eastern Church *sui iuris* has to decide on the admission of married men to holy orders. Currently all Eastern Catholic Churches admit married presbyters, with the exception of the Albanian, Bulgarian, Malabar and Malankara Churches.

As far as the Holy See is concerned, special norms could forbid the admission of married presbyters, especially in territories where the Latin tradition is prevalent. These restrictive norms have been used since 1880 when thousands of Ruthenian faithful migrated to the United States of America together with their married clergy. The Congregation *Propaganda Fide*, with its letter of October 1, 1890, placed an injunction against Ruthenian married priests' settling in the United States. In 1913, the same Roman congregation decreed that among the Eastern faithful of Canada only celibates could be promoted to the holy order of presbyterate.

Between 1929 and 1930, the Congregation for the Eastern Churches, founded in 1917, forbade the ministry of Eastern married priests in some regions. These were the decrees: 1. *Cum data fuerit* of March 1, 1929, for the Ruthenian married clergy migrating to North America; 2. *Qua sollerti* of December 23, 1929, extended the prohibition to all Eastern married clergy migrating to the North and South America, Canada and Australia; 3. *Graeci-Rutheni Ritus* of May 24, 1930, for the Greek-Ruthenian clergy of Canada. The reason for the prohibition was the Latin concern that the presence of a married clergy could have a negative influence on Latin celibate priests and confuse the Latin faithful acquainted only with Latin discipline.

This norm was also extended by the Roman Pontiff to other territories not considered 'Eastern regions,' that is, those places where the Eastern rite was observed since ancient times (*Postquam Apostolicis Litteris* c. 303, §1, 2°). One should also keep in mind that this norm may not be changed without having first heard the local episcopal conference and received permission from the Holy See.

Dimissorial Letters and the Rite of Sacred Ordination

Dimissorial letters are a document issued by one's hierarch/ordinary in virtue of which a candidate may be lawfully ordained a deacon or priest by a bishop other than the bishop who has jurisdiction over him. This document testifies to the ordinand's fitness, completion of studies, freedom from irregularities, and so on.

On occasion, candidates from an Eastern Church may be assigned to the service of a Latin diocese and, in virtue of their diaconal ordination, become ascribed therein. Similarly, Latin candidates may be designated to serve an Eastern area.

The Eastern code c. 752 establishes that "dimissorial letters can be sent from the proper eparchial bishop to any bishop of the same Church *sui iuris*; not, however, to a bishop of a church different than that of the candidate, without the permission of those mentioned in c. 748, §2." In fact, c. 748, §2 prescribes: "An eparchial bishop cannot ordain a candidate subject to him who is ascribed to another Church *sui iuris* without the permission of the Holy See; if, however, it is a case of a candidate who is ascribed to a patriarchal Church (or a major archiepiscopal Church) and has a domicile or quasi-domicile within the territorial boundaries of the same Church, the patriarch (or major archbishop) can also grant this permission."

The Latin code on this matter states: "Dimissorial letters can be sent to any bishop in communion with the Apostolic See except to a bishop of a rite different from the rite of the candidate unless there is an apostolic indult" (CIC c. 1021). "If not impeded by a just cause, the proper bishop is to ordain his own subjects personally; without an apostolic indult, however, he cannot ordain licitly a subject of an Eastern rite" (CIC c. 1015, §2).

Actually, an Eastern eparchial bishop, with the permission of the Holy See or his patriarch or major archbishop, can ordain a Latin cleric subject to him who has been designated to serve his eparchy. In this case, ordination must be conferred according to the Eastern rite; to use the Latin rite requires a special faculty from the Holy See (CCEO c. 674, §2). If the bishop does not intend to obtain such an indult, he must send dimissorial letters to a bishop in good standing of the same rite as the candidate to be ordained.

Furthermore, a Latin diocesan bishop, with permission of the Holy See, can ordain an Eastern cleric subject to him who has been designated to serve his diocese. In this case, ordination must be conferred according to the Latin rite; to use the Eastern rite requires a special faculty from the Holy See (CIC c. 846, §2). If the bishop does not intend to obtain such a faculty, he must send dimissorial letters to a bishop in good standing of the same rite as the candidate to be ordained.

These same norms apply equally to Eastern candidates admitted into a Latin religious institute who are to be advanced to sacred orders, and vice versa. Of course, the permission of the Holy See to licitly admit such a candidate to the novitiate also implies his advancement to sacred orders according to the rite of that institute and by the imposition of the hands of a bishop of the same ritual Church.

See *Incardination/Ascription of Clerics; Sacred Ordination.*

Dispensation from Impediments of Receiving or Exercising Sacred Orders

An eparchial bishop or a major superior (general or provincial) of an institute of consecrated life can dispense his subjects from the impediments of receiving or exercising sacred orders in the following cases:

- a person who has seriously and maliciously mutilated himself or another person, or a person who has attempted suicide;
- a person who has performed an act of orders that has been reserved to those who are in the order of episcopacy or presbyterate while the person either lacked that order or had been forbidden its exercise by a canonical penalty;
- a person who holds an office or position of administration that is prohibited to clerics, for which he must render an account, until he becomes free by relinquishing the office and position of administration and has rendered an account of it;
- a neophyte, unless he has been sufficiently proven in the judgment of the hierarch.

The eparchial bishop or the major superior cannot dispense his subjects if the fact on which the impediment is based has been brought to the judicial forum.

A patriarch can also dispense candidates for orders or clerics who have a domicile or quasi-domicile within the territorial boundaries of the Church over which he presides from the following impediments:

- a person who has committed the delict of apostasy, heresy or schism;
- a person who has attempted marriage, even only a civil one, when he was impeded from entering marriage because he was bound by an existing matrimonial bond, sacred orders or a public perpetual vow of chastity, or because he attempted marriage with a woman bound by a valid marriage or by the same type of vow;
- a person who has committed voluntary homicide or who has procured a completed abortion, and all persons who positively cooperated in either (CCEO cc. 762, 767).

Eastern Deacons

The deacons of the Eastern Churches by their ministry share more fully with the bishops and presbyters in the celebration of the Divine Liturgy and other sacraments, in accordance with the prescriptions of the liturgical books of their own Church *sui iuris*. Unlike the Latin discipline, an Eastern deacon is not an ordinary minister of the sacrament of baptism, but in a necessity he may administer it (CCEO c. 677, §2). Also he cannot be delegated to celebrate a marriage, for every marriage requires the blessing of the priest (CCEO c. 828). Ordinarily, he does not distribute the Divine Eucharist or preach the homily, but, if the particular law of his own Church *sui iuris* provides for it, he may do so (CCEO cc. 709, §1; 614, §4).

When an Eastern deacon, endowed with bi-ritual faculties or adaptation of rite, serves a Latin diocese, he may carry out the functions of the Latin deacon during the Holy Mass, administer baptism, and assist in the marriages of Latin Catholics.

Eastern Minor Orders

In Eastern Churches *sui iuris*, besides bishops, presbyters and deacons, other ministers, constituted in minor orders and generally called minor clerics (*clerici minores*), may be admitted or installed to serve the people of God or to exercise liturgical functions; they are governed solely by the particular law of the proper Church *sui iuris* (CCEO c. 327).

For instance, particular law could establish that a person, through the reception of minor orders, can be ascribed into the local eparchy. In fact, the Eastern code states that, "Through diaconal ordination, one is ascribed as a cleric to the eparchy for whose service he is ordained, unless in accord with the norm of particular law of his own Church *sui iuris* he has already been ascribed to the same eparchy" (CCEO c. 358).

Moreover, by particular law Christian lay persons may carry out some functions of the sacred ministers, like those listed in c. 230, §3 of the Latin code: "When the need of the Church warrants it and ministers are lacking, lay persons, even if they are not lectors or acolytes, can also supply certain of their duties, namely, to exercise the ministry of the word, to preside over liturgical prayers, to confer baptism, and to distribute Holy Communion, according to the prescripts of the law"(See also CCEO c. 403, §2).

Formation of Eastern Candidates to Sacred Orders

In conformity with the teachings of the Second Vatican Council, the Eastern code offers several recommendations regarding the spiritual and liturgical formation of those who aspire to the sacred ministry. First, they are to be formed in such a way that they learn to cultivate in the Holy Spirit an intimate familiarity with Christ and to seek God in all things so that, impelled by the love of Christ the Pastor, they become solicitous to gain all people for the kingdom of God by the gift of their very lives. Second, from the word of God and the sacramental mysteries, they should draw strength daily for their spiritual life and their apostolic work.

Canon 346 sets forth at great length a basic program of formation for Eastern candidates to sacred orders:

- Watchful and constant meditation on the word of God and the faithful explanation of it according to the Fathers of the Church;
- Assiduous participation in the Divine Liturgy, the source and summit of the life of the seminary;
- Learning to celebrate constantly the Divine Praises according to their own rite and drawing nourishment from it for their spiritual life;
- Exercises of piety that are helpful to the spirit of prayer and make for the strengthening and defense of an apostolic vocation, especially those exercises that are commended by the venerable tradition of their own Church *sui iuris;*
- Filial veneration to the Holy Virgin Mary, the Mother of God, whom Christ has made Mother of all.

Among the theological disciplines to be taught in major seminaries, liturgy is to be presented taking into account its special importance as a indispensable source of doctrine and of a truly Christian spirit (CCEO c. 350, §3). Canon 352, §2 then reinforces the point: "Students are to be instructed especially...in the liturgical celebration."

As for the proper formation of deacons not destined for priesthood, c. 354 emphasizes that the traditions of their own Church *sui iuris* concerning the service (*diaconia*) of the liturgy should be respected. Canon 591, 2°, addressing missionary catechesis, urges missionaries to be diligent in ensuring that "catechists be formed is such a way that, as valid cooperators of the sacred ministers, they may be able to discharge their task in the work of evangelization and in liturgical service." Also, in catechetical directories the special character of the Eastern Churches is to be respected, so that biblical and liturgical dimensions ... are highlighted in imparting catechesis (CCEO c. 621, §2).

The 1996 Liturgical Instruction of the Congregation for the Eastern Churches expands on these canons: "It is, therefore, necessary that the liturgical life be celebrated with great care and always in its integral form in Eastern seminaries and in formation institutes of Eastern monks and religious, such that the candidates may be shaped by it and learn it in all its richness and completeness, giving due space not only to the Eucharist but also to the Divine Office. The liturgy is to be the true font of spirituality by which the candidates are formed, the element that unifies all that they learn, and the place in which doctrine becomes celebration of praise and thanksgiving and life is transformed by grace" (LI 71).

Formation of Eastern Seminarians in Latin Seminaries

The Eastern code presents the possibility of erecting, by agreement, a major seminary that serves several eparchies of the same Church *sui iuris* or even of different Churches *sui iuris*, including the Latin Church, that have an eparchy/diocese in the same region or nation (CCEO cc. 332 §2, 333, 343). Even though it is preferable to reserve a seminary for students of one Church *sui iuris,* students of another Church *sui iuris*, on account of special circumstances, can be admitted into the same seminary. This arrangement would constitute an "inter-ritual" seminary.

The Latin code (CIC c. 237) foresees the possibility of erecting an "inter-diocesan" seminary that serves several Latin dioceses, without explicitly mentioning "inter-ritual" seminaries. Nonetheless, even apart from the erection of "inter-ritual" seminaries, it is already a sustained praxis that Eastern seminarians or religious studying for their own eparchies or institutes are sent to Latin seminaries. Inter-ritual seminaries could offer a more effective environment for the education of all seminarians, Eastern and Latin, according to a truly complete Catholic formation.

In general, the formation of students for sacred orders should be characterized by a truly universal spirit through which they are internally prepared to respond in the service of souls everywhere in the world. They are to be instructed about the needs of the entire Church and especially about the apostolate of ecumenism and evangelization (CCEO c. 352 §3; CIC, c. 257, §1). More specifically, in "inter-ritual" seminaries, the Eastern code prescribes that the students be formed in the rite of their own Church *sui iuris*, any contrary custom being reprobated (CCEO c. 343).

From these remarks, it is clear that not only do Eastern students in a Latin seminary remain ascribed to their own Church *sui iuris*, but also the Latin seminary that accepts them, with the exception of its internal rules, is to assure their formation according to their own rite, their own liturgical exercises and their own form of spiritual life. The clause "any contrary custom being reprobated" of c. 343 makes the norm definitive, and, even though there is no equivalent in the Latin code, its import applies equally to the Latin Church, in order to avoid the loss of identity of Eastern students and the 'Latinization' of Eastern clerics.

Seminary rectors and faculty members should very much take to heart the recommendation that the "Christian faithful of any Church *sui iuris*, even the Latin Church, who by reason of their office, ministry, or function have frequent dealings with the Christian faithful of another Church *sui iuris,* are to have an accurate formation in the knowledge and practice of the rite of the same Church in keeping with the importance of the office, ministry or function they hold" (CCEO c. 41).

Some steps, therefore, are necessary for Latin major seminaries dealing with both Eastern and Latin students. The following are only a few suggestions:

- that there be, among the faculty members, some instructors trained in Eastern matters;
- that Eastern authorities, when sending their students to Latin major seminaries, choose those where Eastern formation is readily available;
- that the same authorities, having secured the formation of the first cycle of studies in their own seminaries, choose only those students destined for specialized studies elsewhere;
- that the superiors of Latin seminaries encourage their Eastern students to attend, at least on Sundays and holy days, their respective churches or chapels, if there are any nearby;
- that the same Latin superiors provide some space within the seminary for the liturgical use of their Eastern students (Divine Praises/Liturgy of the Hours, Akathist Hymns, ...).

See *Inter-ritual Seminaries.*

Inter-ritual Seminaries

The Eastern code opens the door to the erection, by agreement, of a major seminary at the service of various Churches *sui iuris* having eparchies in the same region or nation, "so that, whether by the appropriate number of students or the number of properly qualified moderators and teachers, as well as by sufficient material resources, and the best combined efforts, formation is provided for which nothing is left wanting" (c. 332, §2). This norm is not found in the Latin code, but implicitly it is also applicable to it insofar as CIC c. 237 foresees the possibility of erecting an inter-diocesan seminary to serve several Latin dioceses. Even though this Latin canon does not make explicit reference to an inter-ritual seminary, it does not preclude consideration of such an arrangement.

Moreover, c. 333 of the Eastern code states: "Even if it is preferable that a seminary, especially minor seminaries, be reserved to students of one Church *sui iuris*, on account of special circumstances, students of another Church *sui iuris* can be admitted into the same seminary." A similar norm does not appear in the Latin code, but *ex natura rei* one can assert that these Eastern directives apply equally to the Latin Church.

It is already a common praxis, even apart from the erection of an inter-ritual seminary that eparchial or religious students, destined to serve their own eparchies or congregations, study at Latin seminaries. An inter-ritual seminary can offer a propitious occasion to both Latin and Eastern students for a more integral Catholic formation.

See *Formation of Eastern Candidates to Sacred Orders.*

Loss of the Clerical State

Without undermining the theological principle that sacred ordination, once validly received, is never nullified, a cleric nonetheless can lose the clerical state through a judicial sentence or administrative decree that declares the invalidity of his sacred ordination, through the legitimate imposition of the penalty of deposition, or through a rescript of the Holy See or of the competent patriarch (CCEO c. 394).

The patriarch, with the consent of the synod of bishops or, if there is danger in delay, of the permanent synod, can remove a cleric from the clerical state if he has a domicile or quasi-domicile within the patriarchal territory and is not bound by the obligation of clerical celibacy or, if bound, is not seeking a dispensation from this obligation (CCEO c. 397). For example, the patriarch can grant such a rescript to a married cleric.

A cleric who loses the clerical state in accord with the norm of the law loses the rights proper to the clerical state and is no longer bound by any of its obligations. He is forbidden to exercise the power of orders and is deprived by the law itself of all offices, ministries, functions and any delegated power (CCEO c. 395).

On the other hand, except for the case in which the invalidity of sacred ordination has been declared, loss of the clerical state does not bring with it a dispensation from the obligation of celibacy, which is granted only by the Roman Pontiff (CCEO c. 396). By special papal faculty, the Congregation for the Clergy is competent to handle the petitions for such dispensations, including those pertaining to clerics of the Eastern Churches.

OTHER SACRAMENTAL ISSUES

Absolution from Reserved Sins and Censures

Canonical Norm

No sins are directly reserved in the Latin code nor is there foreseen the possibility for such reservation on the part of bishops, but there are serious sins that are also crimes, to which is attached a canonical penalty. Some particularly serious sins have an excommunication attached to them, the strictest ecclesiastical penalty, which prevents a Christian from receiving the sacraments and fulfilling certain ecclesiastical actions, and whose absolution, as a consequence, can only be given by the Pope, the local bishop or those presbyters with such a faculty. Moreover, in the Latin code there are excommunications *latae sententiae* that are reserved to the Holy See for various crimes: one incurs these penalties simply by committing the crime, provided that the law or the precept expressly states this.

The Eastern code, on the other hand, does not have penalties *latae sententiae*: they do not fit in with the genuine Eastern traditions and are alien to the Orthodox Churches. A canonical penalty must be inflicted by means of penal trial as prescribed in cc. 1468-1482. However, the Eastern code has the concept of reserved sins as a pastoral remedy. Canon 727 states: "In some cases, in order to provide for the salvation of souls it may be appropriate to restrict the faculty to absolve from sins and reserve it to a determined authority; this, however, cannot be done without the consent of the synod of bishops of the patriarchal Church (or major archiepiscopal Church) or the council of hierarchs, or the Holy See."

The absolution of sins is reserved because of their particular gravity. However, the eparchial bishop may not reserve the absolution from some sins without the consent of the synod of bishops of the patriarchal Church or the major archiepiscopal Church, or of the council of hierarchs in the metropolitan Churches *sui iuris* or of the Holy See, in all the other cases.

The Eastern code c. 728, states: "§1. Absolution from the following sins is reserved to the Holy See: 1° direct violation of the sacramental seal; 2° absolution of an accomplice in a sin against chastity. §2. It is reserved to the eparchial bishop to absolve from the sin of procuring a completed abortion."

As far as sins reserved *ipso iure*, the *reservatio peccati ratione sui* in the cases mentioned in c. 728, practically speaking, achieves the same disciplinary effect as those that are reserved *ratione censurae* (of the Latin code), since, in both cases, one must have recourse to the Holy See via the Apostolic Penitentiary (PB art. 117-120) or, in the case of abortion, to the eparchial bishop.

Can a Latin confessor absolve an Eastern faithful who has committed a reserved sin or, on the other hand, can an Eastern confessor absolve a Latin faithful who has incurred a reserved penalty for a crime committed? Since it is matter of the spiritual well-being of the faithful, both presbyters, if they have the faculty to hear confessions, may licitly and validly grant absolution. To a repentant faithful the Church cannot delay her forgiveness or the remission of the penalty. As was said, the *reservatio peccati ratione sui* in the mentioned cases of c. 728 has the same disciplinary effect as the *reservatio peccati ratione censurae*, since the confessor must make recourse to the Apostolic Penitentiary or, in the case of abortion of an Eastern Catholic, to the eparchial bishop.

Anointing of the Sick

Both codes prescribe that all priests (*sacerdotes*), and only priests, validly administer the sacrament of anointing of the sick (CCEO c. 739; CIC c. 1003). It is the task of pastors, in virtue of their office (*ex officio*), to administer this sacrament to those committed to their care.

A Latin pastor licitly administers the anointing of the sick to his faithful and also to Eastern Christians who are subject to him (CIC c. 383 §2; CCEO c. 916, §§ 4-5); likewise an Eastern pastor does the same for his parishioners and those Latin Christians who are subject to him (CCEO c. 193 §2). In necessity, any priest of any Church *sui iuris* (including the Latin Church) is permitted to administer this sacrament to any Christian faithful with at least the presumed permission of those mentioned above. As for the administration of this sacrament to baptized non-Catholics, the norms of *communicatio in sacris* are to be applied (CCEO c. 671, §§3-4; CIC c. 884, §§3-4).

The oil for use in the sacrament of the anointing of the sick is to be blessed by the priest who administers the sacrament (CCEO c. 741). The Latin priest uses oil blessed by his bishop, but, in a necessity, he may bless it as part of the celebration of the sacrament (CIC c. 999, 2°).

Communicatio in Sacris

Communicatio in sacris is the sharing in spiritual activities and resources by Catholics with other Christians not in full communion with the Catholic Church. It is distinguished twofold: sharing in non-sacramental liturgical worship (*communicatio in sacris extra-sacramentalibus*), and sharing in sacramental life, particularly the Eucharist (*communicatio in sacris sacramentalibus*). The term "other Christians" applies to Eastern Orthodox, Anglicans, and Protestants. Those to whom the term "Orthodox" is generally applied are those Eastern Churches which accept the decisions of the Councils of Ephesus and Chalcedon. In recent times, however, it has also been applied, for historical reasons, to those Churches which did not accept the dogmatic formulae of one or other of these councils. To avoid confusion, the general term "Eastern Churches" is used to designate all of those Churches of the various Eastern traditions which are not in full communion with the Church of Rome (ED 18, note 28). Other divisions in the West, stemming from the events usually referred to as the Reformation, gave birth to various communions, national or confessional. Among those in which Catholic traditions and institutions in part continue to subsist, the Anglican Communion occupies a special place (UR 13; ED 98, note 107).

Theological Principle

The basic principle of the Catholic discipline of *communicatio in sacris* is formulated by the Second Vatican Council: "Worship in common is not to be considered as a means to be used indiscriminately for the restoration of Christian unity. There are two main principles governing the practice of such common worship: first, the bearing witness to the unity of the Church, and second, the sharing in the means of grace. Witness to the unity of the Church generally forbids common worship, but the grace to be had from it sometimes commends this practice" (UR 8). "The celebration of a sacrament in a concrete community is the sign of the reality of its unity in faith, worship and community life. As well as being signs, sacraments - most specially the Eucharist - are sources of the unity of the Christian community and of spiritual life, and are means for building them up. Thus eucharistic communion is inseparably linked to full ecclesial communion and its visible expression" (ED 129).

The sacraments, which signify and manifest unity, are also means of grace and salvation. This constitutes a valid reason for the Catholic Church to allow in its canonical discipline, by way of exception, sharing in sacramental life, particularly the Eucharist, by Christians of other Churches and Ecclesial Communities, in certain circumstances and under determined conditions.

In applying this mitigated discipline, the Catholic Church also takes into account the degree of communion in ecclesiality and sacramentality of the other Churches or Ecclesial Communities. The degree of communion in the faith with the Eastern Orthodox Churches is very deep, since "through the celebration of the Holy Eucharist in each of these Churches, the Church of God is built up and grows" and "these Churches, though separated, possess true sacraments, above all, by apostolic succession, the priesthood and the Eucharist" (UR 15).

At the same time, the Catholic Church teaches that by baptism members of other Churches and Ecclesial Communities of the West are brought into a real, even if imperfect communion, with the Catholic Church. "But of itself baptism is only a beginning, an inauguration wholly directed towards the acquisition of the fullness of life in Christ. Baptism, therefore, is oriented towards the complete profession of faith, complete incorporation into the institution of salvation such as Christ willed it to be, and finally the completeness of unity which eucharistic communion gives." The Catholic Church believes that these Churches and Ecclesial Communities "have not retained the authentic and full reality of the eucharistic mystery, especially because the sacrament of orders is lacking; nevertheless when they commemorate his death and resurrection in the Lord's Supper, they profess that it signifies life in communion with Christ and look forward to his coming in glory. For these reasons dialogue should include among its subjects the Lord's Supper and other sacraments, worship and the Church's ministry" (UR 22). All this has been happening since the Second Vatican Council.

Canonical Norm

The specific disciplinary norms that regulate the *communicatio in sacramentalibus* are contained in the two codes - CCEO c. 671 and CIC c. 844 - and further clarified by the Ecumenical Directory (nn. 122-136). They may be summarized as follows:

- It is licit for the Catholic Christian faithful, for whom it is physically or morally impossible to approach a Catholic minister, to receive the sacraments of penance, the Eucharist and the anointing of the sick from non-Catholic ministers, in whose Churches these sacraments are valid, provided that the danger of error or indifferentism is avoided.
- The Ecumenical Directory (n.122) recognizes "that Eastern Orthodox Churches, on the basis of their own ecclesiological understanding, may have more restrictive disciplines in this matter, which others should respect." Indeed, "a Catholic who legitimately wishes to communicate with Eastern Christians must respect the Eastern discipline as much as possible and refrain from communicating if that Church restricts sacramental communion to its own members to the exclusion of others" (n.124). Moreover, the same Ecumenical Directory acknowledges that, "since practice differs between Catholics and Eastern Orthodox Christians in the matter of frequent communion, confession before communion and the eucharistic fast, care must be taken to avoid scandal and suspicion among Eastern Christians not following the Eastern usage."
- As for the reception from a minister of another Church or ecclesial community, "on the basis of the Catholic doctrine concerning the sacraments and their validity, a Catholic who finds himself or herself in the circumstances mentioned above (ED 130-131) may ask for these sacraments only from a minister in whose Church these sacraments are valid or from one who is known to be validly ordained according to the Catholic teaching on ordination" (ED 132).
- Catholic priests may lawfully administer the sacraments of penance, Eucharist and the anointing of the sick to Orthodox faithful who ask for these sacraments of their own free will and are properly disposed. In these cases, due consideration should be given to the discipline of the Eastern Churches for their own faithful and any suggestion of proselytism should be avoided (ED 125). As for the Christian faithful of Churches of irregular status (for example, some non-canonical Eastern communities not recognized by the canonical Orthodox Churches), it is not lawful for Catholic ministers to administer the aforesaid sacraments, unless in the judgment of the Holy See they are found to be sacramentally on the same level of the Orthodox Churches, that is, they possess true and valid sacraments.
- For the Christian faithful of other Churches and Ecclesial Communities, note that, in the present state of their relations with the Catholic Church, there is not yet an agreement on the sacraments, especially on sacred ordination. Consequently, the norms on the administration of the sacraments of penance, Eucharist and anointing of the sick are more restrictive. Catholic priests may administer these sacraments to those in danger of death. In other cases, it is strongly recommended that the

eparchial/diocesan bishop, take into account any general norms that may have been established by the synod of bishops or the assembly of hierarchs or the episcopal conference for judging situations of grave and pressing need.

The conditions under which a Catholic priest may administer these sacraments to a baptized person are that (1) he or she is unable to have recourse for the sacrament to a minister of his or her own Church or Ecclesial Community, (2) asks for the sacrament freely, (3) manifests Catholic faith in this sacrament and (4) is properly disposed (ED 131). The observance of these conditions will avoid the illicit praxis of the so-called "mutual eucharistic hospitality" that has arisen in some Catholic circles.

One must keep in mind that Protestant Ecclesial Communities do not understand the sacraments as the Catholic Church does; and so, when Protestant faithful ask for these sacraments from a Catholic priest they are possibly moved by God's grace to accept the Catholic sacramental tenet. But pastoral prudence in this matter is always the mother of safety. Protestant faithful should regularly avail themselves of the ministers of their own Ecclesial Community. Only the physical impossibility of such availability justifies the request to the Catholic priest. Every form of false irenicism and ecumenism must be avoided, and, at the same time, the reasons for the Protestant's request for the sacrament must be prudently considered.

Undoubtedly, if in particular life situations – serious suffering, exceptional hardships, uncommon circumstances (imprisonment, deportation, wars, and so forth) -- these Protestant faithful stand in need of sacraments that are lacking in their own Ecclesial Communities, they could appeal to a Catholic minister. The "serious need," the physical impossibility of approaching their minister, and the free will of the request should be seen as a positive sign of accepting the Catholic sacramental norm. Here the judgment of the local bishop or any episcopal directive is of great assistance. *Salus animarum suprema lex.*

Norms of Particular Law

In this sensitive matter one should follow the relevant norms of particular law established by the local bishops or the legislative organs of the Eastern Churches *sui iuris* and the Latin Church. Such particular norms should be established after consultation with the competent authority, at least local, of the other interested Church or Ecclesial Community to achieve a certain reciprocity. "There should be a certain reciprocity since sharing in spiritual activities and resources, even with defined limits, is a contribution, in a spirit of mutual good will and charity, to the growth of harmony among Christians" (ED 105).

"Catholics ought to show a sincere respect for the liturgical and sacramental discipline of other Churches and Ecclesial Communities and these in their turn are asked to show the same respect for the Catholic discipline. One of the objectives of the consultation should be a greater mutual understanding of each other's discipline and even an agreement on how to manage a situation in which the discipline of one Church calls into question or conflicts with the discipline of another" (ED 107).

Faculty to Administer the Sacrament of Penance

Eastern presbyters who have the faculty to administer the sacrament of penance, by virtue of their office or of a concession of the local hierarch of the eparchy in which they are ascribed or in which they have a domicile, can validly administer the sacrament of penance anywhere to any of the Christian faithful, unless a local hierarch in a special case expressly denies it. They use this faculty licitly when they comply with the norms established by the eparchial bishop and have at least the presumed permission of the rector of the church or, in the case of a house of an institute of consecrated life, of the superior (CCEO c. 722, §4).

Latin presbyters who have the faculty of hearing confessions habitually, whether by virtue of office or by virtue of the grant of an ordinary of the place of incardination or of the place in which they have a domicile, can exercise that faculty everywhere unless the local ordinary has denied it in a particular case (CIC c. 967, §2).

See *Absolution from Reserved Sins and Censures.*

Holy Oils

Holy Oils are a visible sign of the celebration of the sacramental mysteries and are therefore consecrated or blessed by the local bishop. To receive holy oils from the local bishop signifies ecclesial communion with him as the original dispenser or steward of the sacraments. The Latin code states: "In administering the sacraments in which holy oils must be used, the minister must use oils pressed from olives or other plants and, without prejudice to the prescript of c. 999, 2°, consecrated or blessed recently by the bishop; he is not to use old oils unless it is necessary. The pastor is to obtain the holy oils from his own bishop and is to preserve them diligently with proper care" (CIC c. 847). Canon 999 prescribes that any presbyter in a case of necessity can bless the oil to be used in the anointing of the sick, but only in the actual celebration of the sacrament.

The Eastern code does not have a canon equivalent to c. 847. Both codes, however, prescribe that the chrism or holy myron used in the sacrament of confirmation or chrismation must be consecrated or blessed by a bishop even if a presbyter administers the sacrament (CIC c. 880, §2; CCEO c. 693). The Eastern norm adds that this power of consecrating or blessing may be reserved by particular law to the patriarch (or major archbishop or metropolitan *sui iuris*).

As for the anointing of the sick, the Eastern code prescribes that the oil to be used in the sacrament is to be blessed, and, unless the particular law of his Church *sui iuris* determines otherwise, by the priest who administers the sacrament himself (CCEO c. 741). The oil for the anointing of the sick symbolizes a remedy for spiritual and bodily illness and the strength to bear up under evil and receive pardon for sins.

Minister of Holy Communion

The Divine Eucharist is distributed by the priest or, if the particular law of his Church *sui iuris* provides for it, by the deacon as well. The synod of bishops of a patriarchal Church or the council of hierarchs (not each hierarch of the place alone) is free to establish suitable norms according to which other Christian faithful, too, may distribute the Divine Eucharist (CCEO c. 709). By particular law an Eastern Church *sui iuris* may adopt c. 910 of the Latin code: "the extraordinary minister of holy Communion is an acolyte or another member of the Christian faithful designated according to the prescripts of the law, when the need of the Church warrants it and ministers are lacking."

If this particular law does not exist, an Eastern layperson or a person constituted in a minor order should not serve as an extraordinary minister of the Holy Communion, whether in the Eastern Churches or in the Latin Church.

See *Eastern Minor Orders.*

Mixed Marriages

Norms to be Observed

Marriages of Catholics, even if only one party is Catholic, are governed not only by divine law but also by canon law. A marriage between a Catholic and a baptized non-Catholic (Orthodox or Protestant) is governed by divine law, Catholic canon law, the law proper to the Church or Ecclesial Community to which the non-Catholic belongs, if that community has its own matrimonial law, and the law to which the non-Catholic is subject, if the Ecclesial Community to which the person belongs has no matrimonial law of its own (CCEO c. 780; CIC c. 1059; DC art. 2).

Since marriage has been established by God and ordered by his law, it is governed by divine natural or positive law as authentically taught by the supreme magisterium of the Catholic Church. This divine law binds all men and women, baptized or unbaptized. But, because marriage is one of the seven sacraments of the new covenant entrusted by Christ to his Church to confer sacramental grace, it is also governed by canonical norms. By divine institution the Catholic Church has the right to regulate the celebration and administration of the sacraments for its members.

In mixed marriages, the law proper to the Church or Ecclesial Community to which the non-Catholic (Orthodox or Protestant) belongs is also applied. The application of this law, though, regards only ecclesial diriment impediments, not those of divine law: for example, since the Orthodox Churches do not bless marriages of baptized Orthodox with unbaptized, there is no possibility of a dispensation from the impediment of disparity of worship. Moreover, they do not have canonical measures dealing with defective consent, dissolution of bond, or validation of marriage.

Canonical Form Between Catholics and Orthodox

If a Catholic party ascribed to an Eastern Church *sui iuris* celebrates a marriage with a member of an Eastern non-Catholic Church, the form for the celebration of marriage prescribed by law is to be observed only for liceity; for validity, however, the blessing of a priest is required, while observing the other requirements of law (CCEO c. 834, §2). In other words, the marriage is valid whether it has been celebrated by an Eastern Catholic or Orthodox priest.

The Latin code states that "if a Catholic party contracts marriage with a non-Catholic party of an Eastern rite, the canonical form of the celebration must be observed for liceity only; for validity, however, the presence of a sacred minister is required and the other requirements of law are to be observed" (CIC c. 1127, §1). In other words, the marriage is valid whether it was entered before a Latin priest or deacon or before an Orthodox priest.

It should be noted that, for Orthodox Churches, a marriage between an Orthodox and a baptized person, Catholic or Protestant, must be celebrated before an Orthodox priest. Mixed marriages celebrated only in the Catholic Church are not recognized as valid by the Orthodox because of its defective form, and therefore cannot be duly recorded. If some Orthodox Church should in fact recognize such a marriage, it would still exclude the ministration of a deacon or, *a fortiori,* a lay minister.

See *Marriage of Catholics with Divorced Orthodox and Protestants.*

Participation in the Sacraments

Catholics in the Sacraments of any Catholic Church

The Catholic faithful can participate in the Eucharistic sacrifice and receive Holy Communion in any Catholic rite (CIC c. 923). Every Catholic is free to confess his or her sins to a legitimately approved confessor of his or her choice, even to one of another rite (CIC c. 991).

Catholics in the Sacraments of Eastern Orthodox

It is licit for the Catholic faithful, for whom it is physically or morally impossible to approach a Catholic minister, to receive the sacraments of penance, the Eucharist and anointing of the sick from ministers of an Orthodox Church, if necessity requires it or genuine spiritual advantage suggests it and provided that the danger of error or indifferentism is avoided (CCEO c. 671, §2; CIC c. 844, §2). "Error or indifferentism" would imply a certain doctrinal and ecclesial relativism whereby a Catholic thinks that the same means of salvation can be found in equal measure in every non-Catholic Church or Ecclesial Community.

The Ecumenical Directory, however, recognizes that "Eastern Orthodox Churches, on the basis of their ecclesiological understanding, may have more restrictive disciplines in this matter, which others should respect. Pastors should carefully instruct the faithful so that they will be clearly aware of the proper reasons for this kind of sharing in liturgical worship and of the variety of discipline which may exist in this connection" (ED 122). "A Catholic who legitimately wishes to communicate with Eastern Christians must respect the Eastern discipline as much as possible and refrain from receiving communion if that Church restricts sacramental communion to its own members to the exclusion of others" (ED 124).

Moreover, this same n. 124 reasserts: "Since practice differs between Catholics and Eastern Christians in the matter of frequent communion, confession before communion and the eucharistic fast, care must be taken to avoid scandal and suspicion among Eastern Christians through Catholics not following the Eastern usage."

Consequently, one should keep in mind that the canonical norms of the Orthodox Churches, as a rule, do not admit heterodox to their Eucharistic Communion. Catholics who visit or work in Orthodox countries, then, should refrain from sharing in the sacramental life, especially the Eucharist, of their host country.

As far as the Protestant Ecclesial Communities are concerned, Catholics are reminded: "On the basis of the Catholic doctrine concerning the sacraments and their validity, a Catholic who finds himself or herself in case of danger of death may ask for the sacraments only from a minister in whose Church the sacraments are valid or from one who is known to be validly ordained according to the Catholic teaching on ordination" (ED 132).

See *Communicatio in Sacris.*

Sacred Ordination

Episcopal Ordination
Episcopal ordination is reserved, in accord with the norm of law, to the Roman Pontiff, the patriarch, the major archbishop or the metropolitan *sui iuris*, so that no other bishop is permitted to ordain anyone a bishop unless it is previously established that there is a legitimate mandate to do so (CCEO c. 745).

A bishop is ordained by three bishops, except in case of extreme necessity (*extremae necessitatis*). If bishops of the same Church *sui iuris* as the primary ordaining bishop are unavailable, the second and third bishops can be of another Church *sui iuris* (CCEO c. 746). This norm, although not found in the Latin code, applies as well as to the ordination of a Latin bishop with the participation of a second or third Eastern bishop.

Conferral of Other Sacred Orders
Eastern candidates to be ordained by a Latin bishop or vice versa require an indult from the Holy See (CCEO cc. 674; 748, §2; 752; CIC cc. 846; 1015, §2; 1021).

To safeguard the observance of the liturgical rite of each Church *sui iuris,* as its liturgical patrimony, the Eastern code c. 674 prescribes: "§1. In celebrating the sacraments, that which is contained in the liturgical books is to be observed accurately. §2. The minister should celebrate the sacraments according to the liturgical prescripts of his own Church *sui iuris,* unless the law establishes otherwise or he himself has obtained a special faculty."

The Latin code c. 846 similarly states: "In celebrating the sacraments the liturgical books approved by competent authority are to be observed faithfully; accordingly, no one is to add, omit, or alter anything in them on one's own authority. The minister is to celebrate the sacraments according to the minister's own rite."

Both codes, consequently, require that a candidate to the diaconate or presbyterate be ordained by his own eparchial bishop or by another bishop with legitimate dimissorial letters (CCEO c. 747; CIC c 1015, §1).

The Holy See usually grants an indult so that an Eastern candidate for sacred orders may be ordained by a Latin bishop when the ordinand is going to serve in a Latin diocese or when there is no bishop of the same Church *sui iuris* in the area where the candidate resides. The more frequent case occurs usually when Eastern seminarians study in western countries. The same rule applies to a Latin candidate for holy orders.

Accordingly, one must distinguish between the membership (belonging to) of a candidate in his own Church *sui iuris* and his ascription (incardination) to an eparchy or diocese. As a rule, one becomes a member of a Church *sui iuris* with the reception of the sacrament of baptism (CCEO cc. 29-38; CIC cc. 111-112). Ascription (incardination) to an eparchy or diocese, on the other hand, takes place by ordination to the diaconate. Consequently, one should note that an Eastern cleric even though subject to a Latin bishop always remains a member of his own Church *sui iuris.*

Second Marriage as Impediment to Sacred Orders

Since ancient times, the Eastern Churches considered with reservation the second marriage of their faithful and by way of toleration imposed heavy penances on widowed persons who entered a subsequent marriage. Even the ancient praxis of admission to sacred orders of remarried widowers was more stringent and exacting. Saint Basil the Great (+379), while confirming the norm in existence at his time, stated that "the ecclesiastical rule excludes totally from the ministry of the Church those who have entered a second marriage" (canon 12). As a result, it has been customary to refuse access to sacred orders to those who entered marriage twice or those who married a widow.

Today's Eastern code does not make any specific mention about a second marriage or irregularity to receive sacred orders for those legitimately remarried. Canon 6, §2 states: "With the entry into force of the (Eastern) code all customs reprobated by the canons of this code or which are contrary to them, unless they are centennial or immemorial, are revoked." As for 'centennial or immemorial customs,' they are not abrogated, unless expressly revoked by the canons of this code. In fact, c. 764 determines that: "Impediments for receiving or exercising sacred orders cannot be established by particular law; a custom introducing a new impediment established by common law is reprobated."

The non-admission of remarried widowers to sacred orders is indeed an ancient praxis of the Eastern Christian Churches, both Catholic and non-Catholic. This norm, however, is expressly reprobated by the current Eastern code and it cannot therefore be applied: it is not an impediment for receiving sacred orders. Of course, it is up to the local eparchial bishop to ordain a candidate and ascribe him into his eparchy, with due regard for c. 756, which reminds the bishop: "It is not permitted to turn away from receiving sacred orders anyone who is suitable in accord with the norm of law."

Eastern Widower Clerics

All Catholic Churches include sacred orders (episcopate, presbyterate and diaconate) among their matrimonial diriment impediments (CCEO c. 804; CIC c. 1087). The Eastern married cleric (presbyter or deacon) who becomes a widower is not permitted to remarry. Obviously, this is an impediment of ecclesiastical law, which could be dispensed from by competent authority (CCEO c. 795; CIC c. 1078). This norm is ancient in the Church universal; it was sanctioned by the Apostolic Canons (c. 26) and the Ecumenical Councils, and reconfirmed by the sixth canon of the Council in Trullo (691-692): "Whereas it is stated in the apostolic canons that 'From among the celibate men promoted to the clergy, only the readers and cantors may marry,' so do we, observing this, decree that henceforth no deacon nor presbyter, should in any wise be at liberty to arrange for himself a matrimonial union after his ordination; if he dares to do this, he shall be deposed. If anyone entering the clergy desires to be joined in law to a woman, he shall do this before his ordination as deacon or presbyter."

MONASTICS AND OTHER RELIGIOUS

Admission into Religious Institutes of another Church *Sui Iuris*

Principle

In current times it happens more often that Eastern faithful ask for admission into a Latin religious institute. The case arises under two forms: 1) admission into a Latin institute that lacks an Eastern province or house; 2) admission into an Eastern province or house of a Latin religious institute.

The Second Vatican Council and both codes guarantee all Christian faithful freedom to their own spirituality and emphasize the importance of preserving their religious patrimony. Though there are different kinds of life and different roles, there is only one holiness cultivated and lived by Christians according to their own gifts and duties (LG 41). The council earnestly recommends that Catholics, Eastern and Latin, "avail themselves still more of these spiritual riches of the Eastern Fathers which lift up the whole person to the contemplation of the divine" (UR 15). The Eastern code in c. 40, §2, inspired by the Decree on the Eastern Churches (OE 4-6), specifies that "clerics and members of institutes of consecrated life are bound to observe faithfully their own rite and to acquire always a greater knowledge and more complete practice of it." To make this norm effective requires cooperation between Latin religious institutes and the hierarchy of the individual Eastern Churches.

Canonical Norm

In accordance with these guidelines, the Eastern code c. 451, establishes that "No one can be admitted licitly to the novitiate of a monastery of another Church *sui iuris* without the permission of the Holy See, unless it concerns a candidate who is destined for a dependent monastery, mentioned in c. 432, of his or her own Church." This norm is also applied for the admission of Eastern candidates to the novitiate of a religious institute of another Eastern Church *sui iuris* (orders, congregations and societies of common life according to the manner of religious: CCEO cc. 517 §2 and 559 §1). In fact, c. 517 §2 establishes: "No one can be admitted licitly to the novitiate of a religious institute of another Church *sui iuris* without the permission of the Holy See, unless it concerns a candidate destined for a province or house, mentioned in c. 432, of his or her own Church."

It is worth noting that the permission mentioned in canons 451 and 517, §2 is required *ad liceitatem.* On the other hand, the transfer (*transitus*) of an Eastern monk or religious in perpetual vows to a monastery or religious institute of another Church *sui iuris*, including the Latin Church, requires the consent of the Holy See for validity (CCEO cc. 487, §4; 544, §4; 562, §1). Furthermore, the admission to the novitiate of a non-Catholic who has not yet made the profession of the Catholic faith would be invalid (CCEO c. 450, 1°).

The praxis still followed today by some Latin institutes, according to which all Easterners living in prevalently Latin countries and desiring to enter religious life are considered completely free to opt for the Latin or the Eastern rite, is disapproved. It goes without saying that the reception of an Eastern Catholic into a religious institute of another Church *sui iuris* does not involve *eo ipso* his or her ascription to the same Church.

Canon 432, along with related cc. 451, 517, §2, authorizes a monastery *sui iuris* or a Latin religious institute to found, with the consent of the Holy See, a dependent monastery (filial or subsidiary) or an Eastern province or house. The newly erected monasteries are regulated by the law of the Eastern Church *sui iuris* to which they are ascribed. As for the charism and the internal governance of this house or province, the constitutions of the institute are to be observed. Therefore, an Eastern Catholic can join this type of monastery or house of a Latin religious institute without any authorization of the Holy See. The norm of c. 432 does not have a corresponding canon in the Latin code, but it does apply to the Latin Church, as mentioned in the canon. The Holy See is usually solicitous in inviting Latin religious institutes with members coming from Eastern Churches or doing pastoral work among Eastern Catholics to open some dependent Eastern houses or provinces.

Rationale of the Norm

The reason for this norm is to make more difficult the enrollment of good candidates into religious institutes of another rite. It is backing up the directive of the Congregation for Institutes of Consecrated Life and for Societies of Apostolic Life (Circular Letter, *On the Youth of Other Nations in the Monasteries of Spain,* June 26, 1995, Prot. N. 97416/94) which urges that aspirants to religious life, in particular to cloistered institutes, not be sent to far distant places, different in culture and mentality from that of their origin.

It also aims at averting unpleasant situations in the future in which the individuals and their institutes would have a detrimental conflict of conscience. The right to celebrate divine worship according to the prescripts of one's Church *sui iuris* and to follow its spiritual life involves also the duty and obligation of living in accord with the proper ritual traditions. In fact, the traditions of their origin are more consonant with their culture and way of life, unlike those celebrated in a different language and a foreign mentality

Conditions for the Concession of an Indult

The indult for admission into the novitiate of a religious institute of another Church *sui iuris* is obtained from the Congregation for the Eastern Churches by the candidates' major religious superior. The necessary documentation pertaining to the personal identifying data of the candidate, including the certificate of baptism, is to be attached to the petition.

The papal indult authorizing admission into the novitiate allows the candidate to profess religious vows in that institute and, if the candidate joins a clerical institute, to receive sacred orders. At the same time, the candidate is granted adaptation to the rite of that institute. In the case of a Latin institute, that means that the religious can be part of the liturgical, theological, spiritual and disciplinary patrimony of the Latin Church, while always remaining ascribed to his own Eastern Church *sui iuris*. If, for some reason, the religious should leave the Latin religious institute, he will have to observe the rite of his origin. If a candidate was admitted in the novitiate of an institute of another Church *sui iuris* without the permission of the Holy See, he must petition for the juridical regularization of his status.

Recommendations

It is to be hoped for that religious institutes, especially Latin institutes, take steps to include in their constitutions and by-laws an explicit reference to the Eastern code cc. 451; 517 §2 (on the proper juridical admission to novitiate) with appropriate adaptations.

It is also fitting to establish a norm that recognizes that Eastern candidates, legitimately admitted to a Latin institute, always remain ascribed to their own Eastern Church *sui iuris* and are to continue to observe the law of their

Church, without prejudice to the prescriptions of the constitutions and by-laws that regard the internal governance of the same institute.

Eastern candidates should receive an accurate formation on being familiar with the worship and practice of the rite of their Church, without detriment to the obligation of also knowing those of the institute they belong to by their perpetual profession.

The Eastern members of a Latin institute should be sent to the territories of their origin for ministerial practice, as long as they appropriately collaborate with the hierarchy of their own Church *sui iuris*.

In compliance with the CCEO c. 432, it is worth considering the establishment of a house or a province that is ascribed, with the consent of the Holy See, to the Eastern Church *sui iuris*, to which the institute's Eastern members belong.

See *Eastern Houses and Provinces of Latin Religious Institutes.*

Admission of Eastern Non-Catholics into Religious Institutes

Sometimes it happens that Catholic religious institutes, in a spirit of precipitous ecumenism, accept non-Catholic Eastern Christians into their membership. Canonical discipline does not admit of such a praxis. A baptized non-Catholic cannot validly be admitted into a Catholic religious institute, without having first professed the Catholic faith (CCEO cc. 517, §1; 450, 1°). If admission to the novitiate has taken place, the novitiate and the profession are canonically invalid. In this case, the Holy See, that is, the Congregation for the Eastern Churches, must be petitioned to grant a sanation of the canonical situation of this individual, who has to be legitimately received into the Catholic Church as soon as possible, in compliance with CCEO c. 35.

A non-Catholic monk who asks for admission into a Catholic religious institute, after having professed the Catholic faith, is obliged to repeat the novitiate and to profess his vows again (CCEO c. 493, §2).

Latin religious institutes that intend to admit candidates from non-Catholic Eastern Churches into their novitiate who have already professed the Catholic faith should apply the norms pertaining to Eastern Catholic candidates, except for the situation in which candidates have been granted a papal indult allowing them to be directly ascribed into the Latin Church.

Dismissal of Eastern Monks and Religious

Dismissal "ipso iure"

A monk or religious who has publicly rejected the Catholic faith or has celebrated marriage or attempted it, even if only civilly, must be held dismissed from the monastery or religious order/congregation by the law itself (CCEO cc. 497, §1; 551).

In these cases, once the proofs have been collected, the superior of the monastery *sui iuris*, having consulted the council, is to issue a declaration of the fact so that the dismissal is established juridically, and, as soon as possible, the superior is to notify the authority to which the monastery is immediately subject about the matter (CCEO c. 497, §2). For members of religious orders or congregations the competent authority to make the declaration is the major superior, after consulting his council. Religious institutes of pontifical right are subject directly and exclusively to the Holy See; those of patriarchal or eparchial right are directly subject to the patriarch or eparchial bishop (CCEO c. 413).

Expulsion

A monk or religious who is the cause of imminent and most serious external scandal or harm to the monastery or institute can be expelled immediately by the competent authority (CCEO cc. 498, §1; 551).

The superior of a monastery *sui iuris*, with the consent of the council, expels the monk, after divesting him of the monastic habit. In religious orders and congregations the competent authority is the major superior, with the consent of the council. If there is danger in delay and there is not enough time to approach the major superior, even a local superior, with the consent of the council, can expel a member, informing the major superior immediately. The superior of a monastery *sui iuris* or the major superior, if the case warrants it, is to see that the dismissal process progresses in accord with the norm of law or defer the matter to the authority to which the monastery or institute is subject. An expelled member who is in sacred orders is forbidden to exercise the order unless the competent authority decides otherwise (CCEO cc. 498, §§2-3; 551).

Dismissal of Members in Temporary Vows

A monk or religious in temporary vows can be dismissed by the superior of the monastery with the consent of the council. In addition to the conditions that may be established in the typicon or statutes, valid dismissal requires the following:

- the causes for dismissal must be grave, and on the part of the monk or religious also external and imputable;
- the lack of a religious spirit, which can be of scandal to others, is a sufficient cause for dismissal if repeated warnings, along with salutary penances, have been in vain;
- the dismissing authority must know the reasons with certainty, although it is not necessary that they be formally proven. Yet, they must always be made known to the monk or religious, granting him full opportunity of self-defense, and his response is to be faithfully submitted to the dismissing authority. Recourse against the decree of dismissal has suspensive effect (CCEO cc. 499; 552).

Dismissal of Members in Perpetual Vows

To dismiss a monk or religious in perpetual vows, the superior of the monastery *sui iuris* or the general superior are competent, each of them with the consent of the council, which in this case must consist *ad validitatem* of at least five members, including the presiding superior; if the number of ordinary councilors is insufficient or some are absent, others are to be called according to the typicon or the statutes; voting must be by secret ballot (CCEO c.500).

In addition to other conditions that may be established in the typicon or statutes, valid dismissal requires the following:

- the causes for dismissal are serious, culpable and juridically proven along with a failure to reform;
- the dismissal was preceded, unless the nature of the cause for dismissal precludes it, by two warnings, with the formal threat of dismissal, that were in vain;
- the causes were clearly stated in writing to the monk or religious, giving him, after each warning, full opportunity for self-defense;
- the useful time established in the typicon or statutes has elapsed since the last warning.

The written responses of the monk or religious in question are attached to the acts, which are to be submitted to the superior of the monastery or the general superior of the institute. The decree of dismissal cannot be executed unless it is approved by the authority to which the monastery or the institute is subject.

The decree of dismissal is to be intimated as soon as possible to the monk or religious concerned. The latter can, within fifteen days, either have recourse, with suspensive effect, against the decree of dismissal or, unless the decree of dismissal has been confirmed by the Holy See, request that the case be handled judicially. The Holy See or the patriarch, if it concerns a monk or religious who has domicile within the territorial boundaries of the patriarchal Church, deals with the recourse against the decree of dismissal. If the case is to be handled judicially, it is to be dealt with by the tribunal of the authority immediately superior to the one that has confirmed the decree of dismissal. In such case, the superior who issued the decree of dismissal is to hand over the acts assembled in the matter to the same tribunal; the tribunal proceeds according to the canons regarding a penal trial, with no appeal (CCEO c. 501).

As for the dismissal of an Eastern monk or religious admitted licitly into a Latin monastery or institute (CCEO cc. 451; 517), the norms of dismissal of the Latin code must be observed (CIC cc. 694-704). For the dismissal of an Eastern monk or religious ascribed to a Latin dependent monastery, or a house or province of a religious institute, the norms of dismissal of the Eastern code are to be observed (CCEO c. 432).

Juridical Effects of Dismissal

By legitimate dismissal all bonds and obligations arising from monastic or religious profession cease by the law itself (CCEO c. 502). The monk or religious who leaves a monastery or institute legitimately or has been legitimately dismissed from it is not entitled to anything from the monastery or institute for any work performed in it. Nevertheless, the monastery or institute is to observe equity and charity towards the monk or religious who is separated from it (CCEO c. 503).

Moreover, if an ordained monk or religious in perpetual vows has been granted an indult to leave the monastery or institute and return to the world, he cannot exercise sacred orders until he has found a benevolent eparchial bishop to receive him. The eparchial bishop can receive him either absolutely or on an experimental basis for five years. In the first case, the monk or religious is ascribed to the eparchy by the law itself; in the second case, he is ascribed by the law after the completion of the five years, unless he has been expressly dismissed beforehand (CCEO cc. 502; 494).

Dispensation from Vows of Eastern Religious

A religious in perpetual vows is not to request an indult to leave an order or congregation and to return to secular life except for the most serious of reasons. The religious is to present his petition to the superior general, who is to send it, along with a personal opinion and the opinion of his council, to the competent authority. For monasteries and orders, an indult of this type is reserved to the Holy See (the Congregation for the Eastern Churches); but for religious congregations, in addition to the Holy See, the indult can also be granted by:

- the patriarch with respect to all members who have a domicile within the territorial boundaries of the Church over which he presides, after having consulted, if it concerns a congregation of eparchial right, the eparchial bishop;
- the eparchial bishop of the eparchy in which the religious has a domicile, if it concerns a congregation of eparchial right (CCEO c. 549).

An indult to leave a monastery, an order or a congregation has the following canonical effects:

- The indult legitimately granted and intimated to the member, unless it has been rejected by the member in the act of intimation, entails by the law itself the dispensation from the vows and from all obligations arising from profession, but not from the ones that are attached to a sacred order if he is in sacred orders.
- If a religious in perpetual vows and in sacred orders has obtained the indult to leave the institute and to return to the world, he cannot exercise sacred orders until he has found a benevolent eparchial bishop to receive him. The eparchial bishop can receive him either absolutely or on an experimental basis for five years. In the first case, the religious is ascribed to the eparchy by the law itself; in the second case, the ascription occurs after the completion of five years, unless he has been expressly dismissed beforehand (CCEO c. 494).

- For an Eastern monk or religious licitly admitted into a Latin religious institute (CCEO cc. 451; 517), the norms of departure from an institute of the Latin code (CIC cc. 686-693) are to observed; but for an Eastern monk or religious ascribed to a dependent monastery, a province or a house of Eastern Rite of a Latin institute, the norms of dismissal of the Eastern code must be followed (CCEO c. 432).

Eastern Houses and Provinces of Latin Religious Institutes

The presence of Latin religious institutes in regions where, among Christians, the Eastern rites prevail is centuries-old and is becoming ever more intense. In carrying out their many activities these religious institutes are to keep in mind the uniqueness of the particular Churches and adhere more closely to extant canonical discipline.

In the interests of greater efficacy of the apostolate, the Second Vatican Council has strongly recommended that religious institutes and congregations of the Latin rite working in Eastern countries or among the Eastern faithful establish houses or even provinces of Eastern rite as far as is possible (OE 6). The praxis of the Catholic Church since the pontificate of Pope Benedict XV (+ 1922) abundantly demonstrates the existence of a trend in this direction.

In particular, the Eastern code c. 432, inspired by Vatican II (OE 6), points out the possibility of opening a monastery, a house, or a province of a religious institute ascribed to another Church *sui iuris*. A similar norm is not found in the Latin code, but the Eastern code's statement expressly applies to the Latin Church as well (*etiam Ecclesiae Latinae*). Authorization for such an entity is granted by the Holy See upon request of the major superior, who should have secured prior approval from the competent Eastern hierarch. By reason of the indult, the province, house, or monastery established through the formal act of the major superior acquires Eastern legal personality and must observe the liturgical discipline of the Eastern Church. At the same time, they are required to observe the constitutions of the institute, in fidelity to its charism. This kind of institution is subject *ad normam iuris* to the jurisdiction of the local Eastern hierarch who must see to it that possible latinization and ritual sincretism are avoided. These monasteries, houses, and provinces can receive Eastern candidates without any additional permission from the Holy See.

See *Adaptation of Rite; Biritualism.*

Monasteries

Monastery Sui Iuris
A monastery is a religious house in which the members strive for evangelical perfection by the observance of the rules and traditions of monastic life (CCEO c. 433, §1). From the glorious times of the holy fathers, monastic spirituality flourished in the East, and then later flowed over into the West (UR 15).

Historically, the foundation of monasteries is linked to the cenobitic life, that is, life in common (*koinobion*) characterized by strict discipline, regular worship, and manual work. Primitive monasticism was twofold: anchorite, a way of life in which persons withdraw from the world and devote their lives to the praise of God and the salvation of the world through solitude and constant prayer and penance; and cenobitic, with life in common under the regimen of a rule and a superior. Saint Pachomius (290-346) was the author of the first cenobitic rule, which was later developed by Saint Basil the Great (329-379). This form of monastic life quickly spread in Egypt and Palestine, and reached the West as well in the middle of the fourth century through Saint Benedict of Nursia. The rule of Saint Basil, variously applied in Eastern monasteries, was specified by Saint Theodore of Stoudios in Constantinople (759-826) and several monastic communities on Mount Athos in Greece.

In a monastery the members totally devote themselves to divine worship by a life of concealment, having as a motto the monastic rule of *ora et labora* (pray and work). A monastery *sui iuris* is one that does not depend on another monastery and is governed by its own *typicon* or statutes, approved by the competent authority (CCEO c. 433, §2). Any monastery *sui iuris* can have dependent monasteries. Some of these are filial if, in the erection or decree issued according to the *typicon,* they can aspire to the status of a monastery *sui iuris*; others are subsidiary (CCEO c. 436, §1).

Stauropegial Monastery

The term *stauropegial* (*staurepegiacus*) in Byzantine law refers to the ancient rite of the patriarch's dedication and blessing of a monastery by fixing a cross at the site of the altar. The term today is reserved to monasteries immediately subject to a patriarch who has the right to fix a cross (*stauros*) in the foundation of the monastery at its erection. In current Eastern law a stauropegial monastery is erected by a patriarch, after having consulted the eparchial bishop of the place in which the monastery is located, and with the consent of the permanent synod.

The patriarch can grant to a monastery *sui iuris* the status of a stauropegial monastery in the act of erection. In this way the juridic status of a stauropegial monastery is not seen as an exemption from the jurisdiction of the local eparchial bishop but a privilege granted to the monastery, freeing it for all practical purposes from the authority of the eparchial bishop. The stauropegial monastery is directly subject to the patriarch in such a way that he alone has the rights and obligations of an eparchial bishop with respect to the monastery, the members ascribed to it, and the persons who live for an extended period in the monastery (CCEO c. 486, §§1-2; c. 101).

Latin Monasteries with Dependent Eastern Monasteries

Latin monasteries *sui iuris* can, with the consent of the Holy See, establish an Eastern dependent (filial or subsidiary) monastery. In this case, the Eastern dependent monastery must observe the law of the Eastern Church *sui iuris* to which is ascribed, and the internal governance of the dependent monastery follows the prescripts of the *typicon* or statutes of the Latin monastery *sui iuris* (CCEO c. 432).

See *Admission into Religious Institutes of Another Church Sui Iuris; Eastern Houses and Provinces of Latin Religious Institutes.*

Separation of Spouses for Consecrated Life

Both codes establish that a spouse, while the marriage continues to exist, cannot be validly admitted to the novitiate (CIC c. 643, §1, 1°; CCEO c. 450, 6°). A widowed spouse, however, can embrace the consecrated life. The codes also address situations in which the spouses separate while the matrimonial bond endures (CIC cc. 1151-1155; CCEO cc. 863-866). The innocent spouse has the right to sever the partnership of conjugal life in cases of adultery and in situations in which the other spouse is the cause of grave mental or physical danger to the innocent spouse or to the children or otherwise renders common life unduly hard and difficult.

The Eastern code adds that the particular law of the Church *sui iuris* can determine other reasons for separation in keeping with the customs of the people and circumstances of the place (CCEO c. 864, §2). In the Christian East, from ancient times, the choice of consecrated life by a married person with the consent of the other spouse was considered a legitimate cause for separation. Christian history offers several cases of married persons who, by common agreement, interrupted their cohabitation without breaking the marital bond in order to enter monastic life. A recorded example from the tenth century is Saint Nilus of Rossano, Italy, the spiritual founder of the Exarchic Monastery of Grottaferrata near Rome.

Differing from the Eastern directives, the Latin code does not state any other reasons for separation while the bond endures, but, in a particular case, one should not discount the possibility of obtaining a special indult from the Roman Pontiff for just such a purpose.

Synaxes in Religious Orders

The Greek term *synaxis,* in Latin *capitulum* (chapter), designates the assembly of the members of monasteries *sui iuris*, orders, congregations, and societies of common life according to the manner of religious (CCEO cc. 441; 511-512; 557). The power of the superiors of orders and congregations and their synaxes is determined by common law and their typicon or statutes. In clerical orders and congregations of papal or patriarchal right, superiors and synaxes have, in addition, the power of governance for the external and internal forum in accord with the norm of the statutes.

The general synaxis, which is the highest authority in accord with the norm of the statutes, is to be composed in such a way that, representing the entire order or congregation, it becomes a true sign of its unity in charity. Not only provinces and houses, but every member can freely send his wishes to the general synaxis in the manner determined in the statutes.

Transfer of Eastern Religious to another Institute

Canons 487 and 488 of the Eastern code deal with the transfer to another monastery; cc. 544- 545 treat of the transfer to another order or congregation or to a monastery *sui iuris,* and c. 562, §§1-2 of transfer to another society of common life. The legislator discourages unnecessary or useless transfers from one institute to another, demonstrating the influence of the Second Ecumenical Council of Nicaea (787) which established: "It is not right for a monk or a nun to leave his or her own monastery and transfer to another. However should this occur, it is obligatory that hospitality be given, but such a person should not be accepted as a member without the agreement of his or her monastic superior" (can. 21).

As for the authority to permit a transfer from one monastery to another, c. 487 addresses the following cases:

- from a confederated monastery to another monastery of the same confederation: the written consent of the president of the confederation is required;
- from a non-confederated monastery *sui iuris* to another non-confederated monastery *sui iuris*: if both monasteries are subject to the same authority (eparchial bishop, patriarch, Holy See), the consent of the common authority is required; if, however, the monastery to which the transfer is made is subject to another authority (for instance, from a monastery of eparchial right to a monastery of patriarchal or papal right), the consent of the latter authority is also required;
- the patriarch, the eparchial bishop and the president of the confederation cannot give this consent without having consulted the superior of the monastery *sui iuris* from which the transfer is made; if the transfer is to a monastery of papal right, the Holy See is not bound to this consultation, even though it is customarily done;
- from a monastery of an Eastern Church *sui iuris* to a monastery of another Eastern Church *sui iuris*: the consent of the Holy See is also required for validity. This norm is also required for the transfer from an Eastern monastery *sui iuris* to a Latin monastery *sui iuris*, even though there is no specific mention of this in the code. Moreover, this norm is also followed in the case of a monk ascribed to a dependent monastery (see c. 432); for instance, a monk ascribed to an Eastern monastery dependent on a Latin monastery *sui iuris* cannot validly transfer to the Latin monastery *sui iuris* on which the Eastern monastery is dependent without the consent of the Holy See;
- a transfer occurs when the superior of the new monastery *sui iuris*, with the consent of the synaxis, grants admission.

As for the legitimate transfer from one monastery to another, c. 488 of the Eastern code establishes the following:

- one who transfers to another monastery *sui iuris* of the same confederation does not go through the novitiate nor make a new profession;
- one who transfers from one monastery *sui iuris* to another monastery *sui iuris* that does not belong to any confederation or that belongs to a different one shall observe the prescripts of the typicon or statutes of the monastery to which the transfer is made, regarding the obligation to go through the novitiate and make profession. If there is no provision in the typicon, the transfer is effective the day on which the transfer occurs, unless the superior of the monastery requires the person to go through some probationary period, not longer than a year, in the monastery. When the probationary period has elapsed he is to be ascribed permanently into the new monastery by the superior with the consent of the synaxis or is to return to the original monastery.

In a transfer from a monastery *sui iuris* to an order or congregation, cc. 544-545 are to be observed with the necessary adaptations.

The monastery *sui iuris* from which the member transfers keeps the goods that have been already acquired by it because of its members. With respect to the dowry, it belongs to the monastery to which the transfer is made, from the day of transfer, without the revenues that have already accrued.

As for transfer to another order or congregation or a monastery *sui iuris,* cc. 544-545 of the Eastern code establish the following:

- within the territorial boundaries of the patriarchal Church, a member can transfer validly to another order or congregation with the written consent of the patriarch and with the consent of his own superior general and the superior general of the order or congregation to which he wishes to transfer, or, if it concerns transfer to a monastery, of the superior of the monastery *sui iuris;* for the granting of their consent, the superiors need the prior consent of the synaxis;
- a member can validly transfer from a congregation of eparchial right to another religious institute of eparchial right with the written consent of the eparchial bishop of the place where the principal house of the religious institute, to which the member is transferring, is located, once the bishop has consulted the superior general of the congregation from which transfer is being made and has obtained the consent of the superior general of the congregation or the superior of the monastery *sui iuris* to which the transfer is being made. In order to grant this consent, the superiors need the prior consent of their council or, if it is a monastery, of the synaxis;
- in other cases, the member cannot validly transfer to another religious institute without the consent of the Holy See. These other cases involve the transfer from one religious institute to another religious institute

outside the territorial boundaries of a patriarchal Church, except when the transfer is from a congregation of eparchial right to another congregation of eparchial right or to a monastery *sui iuris* of eparchial right;

- for valid transfer to a religious institute, of any type, belonging to a different Church *sui iuris,* including the Latin Church, the consent of the Holy See is required. In this case the Holy See's consent for the transfer (*transitus*) to a religious institute of another Church *sui iuris* does not include the ascription of the religious to the different Church *sui iuris.* For that to take place, one must follow c. 32.

As for the juridical consequences of a valid transfer, c. 545 establishes the following:

- the one who transfers must go through the entire novitiate, unless the superior general or the superior of the monastery *sui iuris*, with the consent of their council, because of special circumstances, reduces the novitiate period, but not less than six months. During the novitiate, while the vows remain in force, the rights and particular obligations that the member had in the previous order or congregation are suspended, and the member is subject under the vow of obedience, to the superiors and director of novices of the new religious institute;
- after completing the novitiate, one who is already professed in perpetual vows publicly makes perpetual profession according to the prescripts of the statutes of the new religious institute. By this profession, the member is fully aggregated to the new institute and, if he is ordained, he is also ascribed to it as a cleric. One, who is only in temporary vows, is to make a temporary profession in the same manner for at least three years, unless the member went through the entire three years of novitiate in the monastery *sui iuris* to which he transferred;
- if a member does not make the profession in the new religious institute, the member must return to the original institute, unless in the interim the time of profession has lapsed;
- regarding goods and dowry, the monastic norms are to be observed, that is, the institute from which the member transfers is keeps the goods that have been already acquired by it because of the member. The dowry belongs to the institute to which the transfer is made, from the day of transfer, without the revenues that have already accrued.

LITURGICAL ISSUES

A-liturgical Days

The Divine Liturgy can be praiseworthily celebrated on any day except those that are excluded according to the prescripts of the liturgical books of the Church *sui iuris* in which the priest is ascribed (CCEO c. 704). The Byzantine tradition during the Great Fast or Lenten Season does not celebrate the Divine Liturgy, but on Wednesdays and Fridays serves the Liturgy of the

Presanctified Gifts. This Liturgy, which does not contain a prayer of consecration, is combined with the daily vespers. Holy Communion may be received from the Eucharist reserved in the artophorion/tabernacle from the previous Sunday's Divine Liturgy. It goes without saying that the Divine Liturgy is celebrated every Sunday.

See *Offering for Celebrating the Divine Liturgy.*

Altar

Ecclesiogical Principle
The Divine Liturgy is to be celebrated in a sacred place, unless in a particular case necessity demands otherwise; in which case, the celebration ought to be offered in a decorous place. The church is the place where a community normally celebrates the liturgical services. Catholic churches are consecrated or blessed edifices that have an important theological and liturgical significance for the Catholic community (LI 102-103; ED 137). The celebration of the Divine Liturgy on a consecrated altar manifests the visible communion with the Catholic Church and the local bishop. Consequently, Catholic churches and altars are generally reserved for Catholic worship.

Canonical Norm
A Catholic priest, Eastern or Latin, may celebrate the Divine Liturgy on the altar of any Catholic Church (CCEO c. 705, §1; CIC c. 932, §2). When doing so, the celebrant must commemorate the bishop of the place where he celebrates. However, for a just cause and with the express permission of the local hierarch, a Catholic priest is permitted to celebrate the Eucharist in the place of worship of some Church or Ecclesial Community that does not have full communion with the Catholic Church so long as there is no danger of scandal (CCEO c. 705, §2; CIC c. 933).

Use of a Catholic Altar by Non-Catholic Ministers
An analogous case would be the use of a Catholic place of worship by non-Catholic ministers for the celebration of their religious worship. The eparchial bishop may permit them to use a Catholic building in compliance with the particular law of his own Church *sui iuris* (CCEO c. 670, §2; ED 137).

Blessings to Non-Catholics

"Blessings ordinarily given for the benefit of Catholics may also be given to other Christians who freely request them, according to the nature and object of the blessing. Public prayers for other Christians, living or deceased, and for the needs and intentions of other Churches and Ecclesial Communities and their spiritual leaders may be offered during the litanies and other invocations of a liturgical service, but not during the Eucharistic Anaphora. Ancient Christian liturgical and ecclesiological tradition permits the specific mention in the Eucharistic Anaphora only of the names of persons who are in full communion with the Church celebrating the Eucharist" (ED 121).

Concelebration

Permitted Between Latin and Eastern Catholic Ministers
Concelebration between bishops and presbyters of different Churches *sui iuris* can take place for a just cause and with the permission of the eparchial/diocesan bishop, especially to foster love and manifest the unity of the Churches. In such situations, the prescripts of the liturgical books of the principal celebrant are to be observed, avoiding all liturgical syncretism, and preferably with all wearing the liturgical vestments and insignia of their own Church *sui iuris* (CCEO c. 701; LI 57). Although this norm does not appear in the Latin code, it is implicitly applicable to Latin bishops and presbyters as well.

Forbidden between Catholics and Non-Catholics
Catholic priests are forbidden to concelebrate the Eucharist Sacrifice/Divine Liturgy with bishops, presbyters or ministers of Churches or Ecclesial Communities that do not have full communion with the Catholic Church (CCEO c. 702; CIC c. 908).

Divine Public Worship

Premise
Divine public worship is the cult carried out in the name of the Church by legitimately appointed persons through acts that are approved by the ecclesiastical authority (CCEO c. 668, §1; CIC c. 834, §2). This worship may be of a non-sacramental kind, or it may involve the celebration of one or more of the Christian sacraments (ED 116).

Competent Authority
For the regulation of divine public worship the competent authorities are the Churches *sui iuris* (CCEO cc. 668, §2; 657; 199, §1). Consequently, c. 668, §2 states that "no other person can add to, remove or modify that which was established by these authorities." In compliance with c. 657, this competence is reserved to:

- in patriarchal Churches to the patriarch with the consent of the synod of bishops of the patriarchal Church;
- in major archiepiscopal Churches to the major archbishop with the consent of the bishops of the major archiepiscopal Church;
- in metropolitan Churches *sui iuris* to the metropolitan with the consent of the council of hierarchs;
- in all the other Churches *sui iuris* this right rests exclusively with the Holy See (Congregation for the Eastern Churches) and, within the limits set by it, to the bishops and their legitimately constituted assemblies.

Patriarchs and bishops are the guardians of the liturgical patrimony of their own Churches. By his own right the patriarch can direct instructions to the Christian faithful of the entire Church over which he presides in order to explain sound doctrine, foster piety, correct abuses, approve and recommend practices that foster the spiritual welfare of the Christian faithful, and issue encyclical letters concerning questions regarding his own Church and rite (CCEO c. 82, §1, 2°-3°). This applies as well to the major archbishop of a major archiepiscopal Church *sui iuris* (CCEO c. 152).

The eparchial bishop is the main guardian of the liturgical patrimony of his own Church *sui iuris*. According to c. 199, §1 "As the moderator, promoter and guardian of the entire liturgical life in the eparchy entrusted to him, the eparchial bishop must be vigilant that it be fostered to the greatest extent possible and be ordered according to the prescriptions and legitimate customs of his own Church *sui iuris*." And c. 201, §2 orders "the eparchial bishop ... to be vigilant lest abuses creep into ecclesiastical discipline, especially concerning the ministry of the word of God, the celebration of the sacraments and sacramentals, the worship of God and the cult of the saints ..." Lastly, c. 415, §1 states that "all the religious are subject to the power of the local hierarch in matters that pertain to the public celebration of divine worship..."

Latin Bishop as Guardian of Eastern Liturgical Tradition in His Diocese

The eparchial bishop to whose care the Christian faithful of another Church *sui iuris* have been committed is bound by the serious obligation of providing everything so that these Christian faithful may retain the rite of their respective Church, and cherish and observe it as far as possible (CCEO c. 193, §1; CIC c. 383, §2). The same obligation applies the Latin diocesan bishop.

Participation of Catholics in Liturgical Worship of Other Christians

Catholics can for a just reason attend the liturgical worship of other Christians and take part in it, observing the norms established by the eparchial bishop or by a higher authority depending on the degree of communion with the Catholic Church (CCEO c. 670, §1). "In liturgical celebrations taking place in other Churches and Ecclesial Communities, Catholics are encouraged to take part in the psalms, responses, hymns and common actions of the Church in which they are guests. If invited by their hosts, they may read a lesson or preach" (ED 118). This is also true for non-Catholic Christians (Orthodox, Anglican, and Protestant) who participate in a Catholic non- eucharistic celebration (ED 119).

Feast Days and Days of Penance

Feast Days of Precept

Feast days of precept common to all the Eastern Churches, besides Sundays, are the Nativity of Our Lord Jesus Christ, the Epiphany, the Ascension, the Dormition of Holy Mary the Mother of God and the Holy Apostles Peter and Paul. The particular law of a Church *sui iuris*, with the approval of the Holy See, may suppress certain feast days of precept or transfer them to a Sunday (CCEO c. 880, §3).

Since the celebration of the Eucharist on the Lord's day is the foundation and center of the entire liturgical year, Eastern faithful should come together on Sundays, as well as feast days of precept, in order to commemorate the suffering, resurrection and glory of the Lord Jesus, by hearing God's word and sharing the Divine Eucharist (SC 106) and, according to the prescripts or legitimate custom of their own Church *sui iuris*, by the celebration of the Divine Praises or Liturgy of the Hours. In order for the Christian faithful to fulfill this obligation more easily, the useful time runs from the evening of the vigil until the end of the Sunday or feast day (CCEO c. 881, §§1-2). For this reason, it is not advisable to organize ecumenical services on Sundays; and one must keep in mind that, even when Catholics participate in ecumenical services or in services of other Churches or Ecclesial Communities, the obligation of participating in the Divine Liturgy on these days remains (ED 115).

Days of Penance

On days of penance the Christian faithful are obliged to observe fast or abstinence in the manner established by the particular law of their Church *sui iuris* (CCEO c. 882; CIC c. 1251).

Observance Outside the Territory of Their Own Church Sui Iuris

The Christian faithful who are outside the territorial boundaries of their own Church *sui iuris* can adapt to the norms about feast days and days of penance where they are staying (CCEO c. 883, §1).

Observance by Inter-ritual Families

In Catholic families in which the spouses are ascribed to different Churches *sui iuris*, it is permissible to observe the norms of one or the other Church *sui iuris* in the matter of feast days and days of penance (CCEO c. 883, §2).

Liturgical Books

Liturgical books are published by the competent authority and prescribed for the exclusive use of the liturgy of the Church. The approval of liturgical books, after prior review (*praevia recognitio*) of the Holy See, is reserved in patriarchal Churches to the patriarch with the consent of the synod of bishops of the patriarchal Church; in major archiepiscopal Churches to the major archbishop with the consent of the bishops of the major archiepiscopal Church; in metropolitan archiepiscopal Churches *sui iuris* to the metropolitan archbishop with the consent of the council of hierarchs (CCEO c. 657). In all other Churches *sui iuris*, this right rests exclusively with the Holy See, and, within the limits set by it, to the bishops and their legitimately constituted assemblies.

Prior review of the Holy See is essentially an attentive examination from the doctrinal point of fidelity to the ritual tradition insofar as *lex orandi* is *lex credendi*, that is, the law of praying is the law of believing, prayers express beliefs. It is an act that falls within the jurisdiction of the Supreme Magisterium of the Church, not the single bishop. The competent dicastery that grants the *recognitio* for liturgical books is the Congregation for the Eastern Churches with the previous permission (*nihil obstat*) of the Congregation for the Doctrine of the Faith.

See *Divine Public Worship*.

Offering for Celebrating the Divine Liturgy

Priests are permitted to receive the offerings that the Christian faithful, following a custom approved by the Church, give for celebrating the Divine Liturgy for their intentions. It is also permissible, if established by legitimate custom, to receive offerings for the Liturgy of the Pre-Sanctified Gifts and for the commemorations in the Divine Liturgy (CCEO c.715). In the Byzantine tradition, the Liturgy of the Pre-Sanctified Gifts is celebrated during the Great Fast or Lent. It is so named because the bread and wine used in this liturgical service have been consecrated on the previous Sunday.

The Eastern code earnestly urges eparchial bishops to introduce, insofar as possible, the practice in which the only offerings received on the occasion of the Divine Liturgy are made by the Christian faithful of their own accord. Even without an offering, priests should celebrate the Divine Liturgy readily for the intentions of the Christian faithful, especially of the poor (CCEO c. 716).

If Eastern priests accept offerings for the Divine Liturgy from the Christian faithful of another Church *sui iuris*, they are bound by the serious obligation of observing the norms of that Church regarding those offerings, unless it stated otherwise by the donor (CCEO c. 717). The norms of the Latin Church with regard to these offerings are set forth in Book Four: *The Sanctifying Function of the Church* (CIC cc. 945-958):

- Any appearance of trafficking or trading is to be excluded entirely from the offerings for Masses.
- Separate Masses are to be offered for the intentions of those for whom a single offering, although small, has been given and accepted.
- A person obliged to celebrate and apply Mass for the intention of those who gave an offering is bound by the obligation even if the offering received has been lost through no fault of his own.
- If a sum of money is offered for the application of Masses without an indication of the number of Masses to be celebrated, the number is to be computed on the basis of the amount established in the place where the donor resides, unless the intention of the donor is legitimately presumed different.

- A priest who celebrates several Masses on the same day can apply each to the intention for which the offering was given, but subject to the rule that he is to keep the offering for only one Mass and transfer the others to the purposes prescribed by the bishop, while allowing for some recompense by reason of an extrinsic title. A priest who concelebrates a second Mass on the same day may not accept an offering for it under any title.
- No one is permitted to accept more offerings for Masses to be celebrated by himself than he can satisfy within a year.
- A person who intends to entrust to others the celebration of Masses is to arrange their celebration as soon as possible by priests acceptable to him, provided that he is certain that they are above reproach. He must transfer the entire offering received unless it is certain that the excess over the sum fixed in the diocese was given for him personally. He is also obliged to see to the celebration of the Masses until he learns that the obligation has been accepted and the offering received.
- The time within which Masses must be celebrated begins on the day the priest who is to celebrate them received the donation unless it is otherwise evident.
- Those who entrust to others Masses to be celebrated are to record in a book without delay both the Masses which they received and those which they transferred to others, as well as the offerings.
- Every priest must note accurately the Masses which he accepted to celebrate and those which he has satisfied.

Pascha/Easter

The Vatican II Decree on the Eastern Churches teaches: "Until we reach the greatly desired agreement among all Christians about the one day on which the feast of Pascha/Easter should be celebrated, in the meantime in order to promote unity among Christians living in the same region or country, there is entrusted to the patriarchs or the highest ecclesiastical authorities in the locality the task of reaching a unanimous agreement, after discussion with all concerned, to keep Pascha/Easter on the same Sunday" (OE 20; also Constitution on the Sacred Liturgy, *Appendix Concerning the Revision of the Calendar*).

The 1996 Liturgical Instruction clarifies it further: "Until the time in which all Christians reach the desired agreement of fixing one Sunday for the common celebration of the Pascha/Easter feast, the practice, already in use among some Catholic communities living in countries of Orthodox majority, will be encouraged to celebrate Pascha/Easter on the Sunday in which it is celebrated by the Orthodox ... This practice, in addition to being a sign of ecumenical fraternity, allows the Catholic faithful to enter harmoniously in the common spiritual climate, which often also marks civilian life, avoiding inappropriate dissonance" (LI 36).

Places of Worship Made Available to Other Christians

Catholic churches are consecrated or blessed buildings that have an important theological and liturgical significance for the Catholic community. They are therefore generally reserved for Catholic worship. If, however, priests, ministers or communities not in full communion with the Catholic Church do not have a facility or liturgical objects needed for the worthy celebration of their religious ceremonies, the diocesan bishop may allow them the use of a church or a Catholic edifice and also lend them what may be necessary for their services. Under similar circumstances, permission may be given to them for interment or for the celebration of services at Catholic cemeteries (ED 137; CCEO c. 670, §2).

Undoubtedly, these norms serve the purpose of modern ecumenical needs. It is hoped, however, that there will be reciprocal agreements with other Christian leaders to meet the pastoral needs of Catholics who may themselves be without a place of worship.

HIERARCHS

Assemblies of Hierarchs of Several Churches *Sui Iuris*

The Eastern code in several canons exhorts the hierarchs of the various Churches *sui iuris* who exercise their power in the same territory, to promote a unity of action among themselves. This is a type of inter-ecclesial collaboration to discuss pastoral issues and other matters that concern the entire Church over which they preside. In this way unity among these ecclesial communities is strengthened and their sense of belonging to the same Catholic family is also promoted (CCEO cc. 84; 202).

Canon 322 of the Eastern code states that, where it seems advisable in the judgment of the Holy See, periodic assemblies are to be held of patriarchs, metropolitans of metropolitan Churches *sui iuris*, eparchial bishops, and other local hierarchs of various Churches *sui iuris*, including the Latin Church, who exercise their authority in the same nation or region. These assemblies are to be convoked at regular intervals by the patriarch or another competent authority. The purpose of these meetings is that, by sharing the insights of wisdom born of experience and by the exchange of views, the pooling of their resources will promote the common good of the Churches – fostering unity of action, facilitating common projects, readily promoting the good of religion, and safeguarding ecclesiastical discipline more effectively.

The competence of the assembly of hierarchs is varied: it extends to common matters such as the erection of national associations, the constitution of regional and national ecclesiastical tribunals, the relationship with Orthodox Christians, and so on. Its decisions have legal force in accordance with the statutes approved by the Holy See.

Currently the following assemblies of hierarchs are complying with said norm: the Assembly of the Catholic Hierarchy of Egypt, the Assembly of the

Catholic Patriarchs and Bishops in Lebanon, the Assembly of the Catholic Hierarchy in Syria, the Assembly of the Catholic Ordinaries of Holy Land, the Assembly of the Catholic Bishops of Iraq, the Iranian Episcopal Conference.

Assembly of the Catholic Patriarchs of the East

The Assembly of the Catholic Patriarchs of the East was established in 1991, after the promulgation of the Code of Canons of the Eastern Churches, in accordance with c. 322. According to its statutes, approved by all the patriarchs on October 18, 2000, the nature of this assembly is to be a sign and instrument of patriarchal collegiality and communion among the Catholic Churches of the East within the Church universal. Its goals pertain to common pastoral matters, the coordination of pastoral activities, the promotion of justice and peace, the acknowledgment and respect of human rights, and the fostering of ecumenical and interreligious dialogue. The members of this assembly are all the Catholic Patriarchs of the East who annually gather in ordinary session, and, when necessary, in other extraordinary sessions.

Assent of the Roman Pontiff to the Election of Eastern Bishops

Within the territory of a patriarchal or major archiepiscopal Church, bishops are designated by canonical election. Only the members of the synod of bishops of a patriarchal or major archiepiscopal Church may propose candidates suitable for the episcopal office. The synod of bishops examines the names of the candidates and can elect one for a determined see or compose by secret ballot a list of candidates suitable for the office. The synodal decision is then presented through the Congregation for the Eastern Churches to the Roman Pontiff. The Pope may give his assent to the election of each candidate or deny it. By such decision the Roman Pontiff, as the head of the college of bishops, expresses his own confirmation of the suitability of the candidates proposed. The assent of the Roman Pontiff to the list of the suitable candidates, once given, is valid until its explicit revocation. When a suitable candidate has already received such papal assent, and is then elected for a determined see, no further assent is required.

See *Election of Eastern Bishops.*

Bishops of the Eastern Churches

Eparchial Bishops Within and Outside Their Churches' Territory

The eparchial bishop, to whom the eparchy has been entrusted to shepherd in his own name, governs as the vicar and legate of Christ; the power, which he exercises personally in the name of Christ, is proper, ordinary, and immediate, although by the supreme authority of the Church its exercise is ultimately regulated and can be circumscribed within certain limits for the benefit of the Church and the Christian faithful (CCEO c. 178).

Bishops constituted outside the territorial boundaries of the patriarchal or major archiepiscopal Church have all the synodal rights and obligations of the other bishops of the same Church (CCEO c. 150, §1). All and only the bishops of the patriarchal or major archiepiscopal Church, wherever they are constituted, are to be convoked to the synod of bishops of the same Church. Particular law can restrict the deliberative vote of titular bishops and eparchial bishops who are constituted outside the territorial boundaries, without prejudice to the canons on the election of the patriarch or major archbishop, bishops and candidates for the episcopal office (CCEO c. 102, §§1-2).

Coadjutor Bishops

If the pastoral needs of the eparchy requires it, a coadjutor bishop can be appointed *ex officio* with the right of succession and endowed with special powers (CCEO c. 212, §1). A coadjutor bishop is a titular bishop who is not assigned a titular see but given the title of the see to which he has the right of succession (*Communicationes* 9 [1977] 223). Within the territorial boundaries of the patriarchal or major archiepiscopal Church, the patriarch or major archbishop is competent, with the consent of the synod of bishops, to appoint a coadjutor bishop.

The rights and obligations of a coadjutor bishop are established in common law and supplemented in his letter of canonical appointment. The patriarch or major archbishop who appoints the coadjutor determines his rights and obligations after consulting with the permanent synod; if a coadjutor bishop is to be endowed with all the rights and obligations of an eparchial bishop, the consent of the synod of bishops is required (CCEO c. 213).

The coadjutor bishop takes the place of the eparchial bishop when the latter is absent or impeded. The coadjutor must be appointed protosyncellus, and the eparchial bishop is to commit to him, in preference to others, those matters which by law require a special mandate. Inasmuch as he is called to share in the concerns of the eparchial bishop, the coadjutor bishop is to exercise his office so that in all matters he acts in full agreement with him (CCEO c. 215). Upon the vacancy of the eparchial see, the coadjutor bishop, provided that he has already taken canonical possession of his office, becomes by the law itself the administrator of the eparchy until his enthronement as eparchial bishop (CCEO c. 222).

Auxiliary Bishops

If the pastoral needs of the eparchy suggest it, one or several auxiliary bishops are to be appointed at the request of the eparchial bishop (CCEO c. 212, §1). Within the territorial boundaries of the patriarchal or major archiepiscopal Church, the patriarch or major archbishop is competent, with the consent of the synod of bishops, to appoint an auxiliary bishop. The rights and obligations of the auxiliary bishop are those established in common law. If there is no coadjutor bishop in the eparchy, the auxiliary bishop is to be appointed protosyncellus; if there are several, the eparchial bishop is to appoint one of them protosyncellus and the others syncelli (CCEO c. 215, §2).

The auxiliary bishop, inasmuch as he is called to share in the concerns of the eparchial bishop, is to exercise his office so that in all matters he acts in full agreement with him.

Curial Bishops

The patriarch or major archbishop, as "father and head" of his patriarchal or major archiepiscopal Church, can see to it that certain bishops, though no more than three, are elected for the patriarchal or major archiepiscopal curia by the synod of bishops according to the norm of the law (CCEO c. 87). One must always keep in mind the difference between auxiliary bishops of the patriarchal or major archiepiscopal eparchy and bishops of the curia. The curial bishops help the patriarch or major archbishop in the exercise of his functions, but, insofar as his power is personal, he cannot constitute a vicar for the entire patriarchal or major archiepiscopal Church nor can he delegate his power to someone for all cases (*ad universitatem casuum*) (CCEO c. 78, §1).

Emeriti Bishops

An eparchial bishop, whose resignation from office has been accepted, receives the title of eparchial bishop emeritus of the eparchy he governed. He can retain a residence in that eparchy unless in certain cases due to special circumstances the Holy See provides otherwise or, if it is an eparchy within the territorial boundaries of a patriarchal or major archiepiscopal Church, the patriarch or major archbishop does so with the consent of the synod of bishops. The synod of bishops of the patriarchal or major archiepiscopal Church must see to it that provision is made for the suitable and dignified support of the bishop emeritus.

Transfer of Bishops

When transferring to another eparchial see, the eparchial bishop must take canonical possession of the new eparchy within two months of the notification of the transfer. In the interim, in the former eparchy he has the rights and obligations of the administrator of the eparchy (CCEO c. 223). Within the territorial boundaries of a patriarchal or major archiepiscopal Church, for a serious reason the patriarch or major archbishop can, with the consent of the synod of bishops, transfer a metropolitan, eparchial bishop or titular bishop to another metropolitan, eparchial or titular see; if the transferred bishop refuses, the synod of bishops is to resolve the matter or defer to the Roman Pontiff (CCEO c. 85, §2, 2°).

See *Election of Eastern Bishops; Sacred Ordination.*

Canonical Provision of Bishops

An office cannot be acquired validly without canonical provision (CCEO c. 938; CIC c. 146), that is, the juridical act by which functions attached to it are ascribed to a physical person by law or by a competent authority.

Canonical provisions are made in any of the following ways: free conferral, election, postulation (CCEO c. 939; CIC c. 147).

Within the patriarchal territory, the eparchial bishop, elected according to the norm of the law (cc. 182-186), takes canonical possession of his eparchy by a legitimately conducted enthronement, during which the patriarchal letter of canonical provision is publicly read (CCEO cc. 86, §1; 189, §1). Outside the territorial boundaries of a patriarchal Church, eparchial bishops appointed by the Roman Pontiff according to c. 149 take canonical possession of their eparchies by a legitimately conducted enthronement, during which the papal letter of canonical provision is publicly read, usually by the local Apostlic Nuncio.

Before enthronement the eparchial bishop may not involve himself in the governance of the eparchy in virtue of any title, either personally or through others (CCEO c. 189, §3). All these norms are also applicable to the bishops of the major archiepiscopal Churches.

In metropolitan Churches *sui iuris*, eparchial bishops appointed by the Roman Pontiff in accordance with c. 168 take canonical possession of their eparchies by a legitimately conducted enthronement by the metropolitan archbishop, during which the papal letter of canonical provision is publicly read.

See *Bishops of the Eastern Churches; Metropolitans of Churches Sui Iuris; Eastern Ordinariates; Competence of the Patriarch on Canonical Provisions in His Territory; Election of Eastern Bishops; Exarchy(Vicariate).*

Competence of the Patriarch on Canonical Provisions in his Territory

The Second Vatican Council decrees that "The patriarchs with their synods make up a higher tribunal for all matters concerning the patriarchate, including the right of setting up new eparchies and of appointing new bishops of their own rite within the boundaries of their own patriarchal territory, without prejudice to the inalienable right of the Roman Pontiff of intervening in individual cases" (OE 9).

Following this principle, the Eastern code c. 85 establishes that "for a serious reason the patriarch can, with the consent of the synod of bishops of the patriarchal Church and having consulted the Holy See, erect provinces and eparchies, modify their boundaries, unite, divide, and suppress them, and modify their eparchial status and transfer eparchial sees." This norms is also applicable to major archiepiscopal Churches or major archbishops (can. 152).

The "serious reason" may be the pastoral well-being of the faithful, or other reasons of civil, cultural, economic and administrative order, or the particular importance of a see. Previous consultation is necessary so that the Holy See not only is informed but also can express its weighty opinion on acts of particular importance in the life of the patriarchal Churches. The advice given by the Holy See could be of assistance to the patriarch and his synod in avoiding unnecessary complications.

Consultation is not a mere formality but a legal element for validity of the very same juridic acts of the patriarch (CCEO c. 934, §2, 2°) and should precede the issuance of any patriarchal decree and its related promulgation. Although the patriarch is not obliged to accept the opinion of the Holy See, nonetheless he is not to act contrary to that opinion without a reason that he judges to be overriding (CCEO c. 934 §2, 3°).

Within his territory, the patriarch, with the consent of the synod of bishops of the patriarchal Church, is competent to give an eparchial bishop a coadjutor or auxiliary bishop and, for a grave reason, to transfer a metropolitan, eparchial bishop or titular bishop to another metropolitan, eparchial or titular see. If any of these refuse, the synod of bishops of the patriarchal Church is to resolve the matter or defer it to the Roman Pontiff (CCEO c. 85, §2). The patriarch can also, with the consent of the permanent synod, erect, modify and suppress exarchies.

Upon the execution of these juridic acts, the patriarch is to inform the Holy See as soon as possible. This information helps to publicize the news through the Vatican periodicals *L'Osservatore Romano* and *Acta Apostolicae Sedis*. All this is also applicable to the major archbishop of a major archiepiscopal Church.

See *Congregation for the Eastern Churches.*

Conferences of Bishops

A conference of bishops, a permanent institution of the Latin Church, is a group of bishops of a particular nation or territory who jointly exercise certain pastoral functions for the Christian faithful of their nation or territory in order to promote the greater good which the Church offers to humanity, especially through forms and programs of the apostolate fittingly adapted to the circumstances and place, according to the norm of law (CIC c. 447).

The Decree on the Pastoral Office of Bishops in the Church (*Christus Dominus*) foresees in its first chapter that "the pastors of the Church should be reorganized in a way more appropriate to the needs of our own times and of different regions and rites"(CD 38).

The Latin code c. 450, §1 states that "to a conference of bishops ... ordinaries of another rite can also be invited though in such a way that they have only a consultative vote unless the statutes of the conference of bishops decree otherwise." This canon leaves to the national conference of bishops the decision about whether or not to invite the Eastern hierarchs, and, if so, whether they are to have a deliberative vote or not. The statutes of the conference of bishops, which are approved by the Holy See, should settle the matter. As a rule, Eastern bishops are normally associated with the Latin Episcopal conference as members with rights and duties.

A typical inter-ritual structure, like the assemblies of hierarchs of several Churches *sui iuris*, has been adopted by the conference of bishops from Romania, Ethiopia and Eritrea, Bulgaria, Turkey, India, and Greece.

Council of Hierarchs of a Metropolitan Church *Sui Iuris*

The council of hierarchs of a metropolitan Church *sui iuris* is composed of all the bishops under it and follows the norms of CCEO cc. 155-173. All and only the ordained bishops of the metropolitan Church *sui iuris*, wherever they are constituted, must be called to the council of hierarchs. Bishops of another Church *sui iuris*, even of the Latin Church, can be invited as guests only if the majority of the members of the council of hierarchs agrees. Eparchial bishops and coadjutor bishops have a deliberative vote in the council of hierarchs; the other bishops of the metropolitan Church *sui iuris* can have this vote if this is expressly established in the particular law.

The council of hierarchs has power to enact laws and norms, including those matters in which the common law remits the matter to the particular law of a Church *sui iuris*. The metropolitan is to inform the Holy See as soon as possible of the laws and norms enacted by the council of hierarchs. Laws and norms cannot be validly promulgated before the metropolitan has written notification from the Holy See of the reception of the acts of the council. The metropolitan is also to inform the Holy See of other acts of the council of the hierarchs.

The metropolitan is to see to it that the laws of the council of hierarchs are promulgated and its decisions published. Without prejudice to the canons that deal expressly with the administrative acts of the metropolitan who presides over a metropolitan Church *sui iuris*, it is also his responsibility to carry out, with the consent of the council of hierarchs, those administrative acts that are committed by common law to the superior administrative authority of a Church *sui iuris*.

In regard to the nomination of the metropolitan and bishops, the council of hierarchs is to compile for each position a list of at least three of the more suitable candidates and send it to the Holy See, observing secrecy even toward the candidates. In order to compile this list, the members of the council of hierarchs, if they consider it opportune, can inquire of some presbyters or other Christian faithful who are outstanding in wisdom for their opinion about the needs of the Church and the special qualities of the candidate to the episcopate.

See *Metropolitans of Churches Sui Iuris*.

Eastern Ordinariates

Eastern (Oriental) ordinariates are geographical ecclesiastical structures established for Eastern Catholic communities lacking their own local hierarchy. Heading the ordinariate is a prelate with the title of *ordinary*, appointed by the Holy See, with jurisdiction over the Eastern Catholics lacking their own bishop. Eastern ordinariates were established by the apostolic letter *Officium supremi apostolatus* of Pope Pius X on July 15, 1912.

The *Annuario Pontificio 2008* (Vatican Yearbook 2008) lists the following *Ordinariati per Fedeli Orientali* (pages 1058-1062): Argentina, Austria, Brazil, Eastern Europe, France, Poland, and Romania.

Eastern Patriarchs

The Second Vatican Council reminds us that "The patriarchal function has been flourishing in the Church from the earliest times, already recognized by the first ecumenical councils" (OE 7). A patriarch is "head and father" of his patriarchal Church. Some of these patriarchal Churches boast of having been founded by the apostles themselves. Each patriarch is simultaneously bishop of his own eparchy and local hierarch of the territories of the patriarchal Church that are not constituted into ecclesiastical territorial divisions (CCEO c. 101).

A patriarch has power, in accordance with extant law, over all bishops, including metropolitans, and other Christian faithful of the Church over which he presides (CCEO c. 56). He can validly exercise this power within the territorial boundaries of the patriarchal Church unless the nature of the matter or the common or particular law establishes otherwise (CCEO c. 78, §2).

Outside the territorial boundaries of the Church over which he presides, the patriarch has the right and obligation (*ius vigilantiae*) to seek appropriate information concerning the Christian faithful (CCEO cc. 148; 193). For example, eparchial bishops who appoint presbyters for the care of the Christian faithful of patriarchal Churches are to draw up a plan in consultation with their respective patriarchs. If the latter agree, they are to act on their own authority and inform the Holy See; should the patriarchs disagree for whatever reason, the matter is to be referred to the Holy See (CCEO c. 193, §3).

A patriarch is elected by the synod of bishops of the patriarchal Church. Once the synod has been canonically convoked and two-thirds of the bishops obliged to attend are in fact present in the designated place, the synod is to be declared canonical and can proceed with the election. Whoever obtains two-thirds of the votes is elected, unless particular law provides that, after an appropriate number of ballots (at least three), an absolute majority of the votes suffices. If the election is not brought to completion within fifteen days from the opening of the synod, the matter devolves to the Roman Pontiff (CCEO c. 72).

Even though this canon does not specify the nature of the papal action in the matter, a few papal interventions that have occurred since the promulgation of the code lead one to surmise that the Roman Pontiff can call another synod. This does not, however, preclude the possibility of a direct patriarchal designation: The principle of the conciliar Decree on the Eastern Churches (OE 9), which safeguards the right of the Roman Pontiff to intervene in individual cases could be applied in this particular case.

If the one elected is already an ordained bishop, the synod proceeds with his proclamation and enthronement as patriarch (CCEO c. 75). The synod is also to inform the Roman Pontiff by a synodal letter that the election and enthronement have been canonically carried out, and the new patriarch must request ecclesiastical communion from the pope, as successor of Peter and head of the college of bishops.

Since the pontificate of Pope Innocent III (+ 1216), the Latin pallium was conferred on all Eastern patriarchs as a further symbol of their communion with the Roman See. Pope John Paul II (+ 2005) replaced this practice with a Eucharistic concelebration of the Roman Pontiff with the newly-elected patriarch.

Within the territorial boundaries of the Church over which he presides, the Eastern patriarch possesses ample powers, clearly defined in the Fourth Title (cc. 78-101) of the Code of Canons of the Eastern Churches.

- He has competence to enact decrees that determine the methods to be observed in applying the law or urge the observance of common and particular laws; to issue encyclical letters, instructions and exhortations to the entire patriarchal Church; to promulgate disciplinary norms and decisions established by the synod of bishops; to conduct pastoral visitations in the eparchies of his patriarchal Church; to exercise vigilance over the proper administration of all ecclesiastical property, with due regard for the primary obligation of the individual eparchial bishop.
- With the consent of the synod of bishops of the patriarchal Church and consultation with the Holy See, the patriarch can erect provinces and eparchies, and suppress them, and modify their hierarchical status and transfer eparchial sees. With the same synodal consent, the patriarch is competent to give an eparchial bishop a coadjutor bishop or an auxiliary bishop; for a grave reason, to transfer a metropolitan, eparchial bishop or titular bishop to another metropolitan, eparchial or titular see; if any of these refuse, the synod of bishops is to resolve the matter or defer it to the Roman Pontiff.
- The patriarch is also competent to give to a metropolitan or bishop a patriarchal letter of canonical provision, similar to the papal bull for Latin bishops and the Eastern bishops outside the territory of their patriarchal or major archiepiscopal Churches. Moreover, he is to ordain and enthrone all the metropolitans and bishops of his patriarchal Church.
- The patriarch, with the consent of the synod of bishops and the prior assent of the Roman Pontiff, can enter into agreements with civil authorities that are not contrary to the law established by the Holy See. At the same time, the patriarch represents the patriarchal Church in all its juridic affairs.

See *Competence of the Patriarch on Canonical Provisions in His Territory.*

Eastern Patriarchs in the College of Cardinals

The Latin code c. 350 §3 states that Eastern patriarchs can be made members of the College of Cardinals and, contrary to the other cardinals, have their own patriarchal see as their title. This norm does not appear in the Eastern code.

Historically, the institution of the cardinalate is linked to the presbyterium of the Church of Rome. The cardinals were chosen from the presbyters of the titular or quasi-parochial churches of Rome, the regional and palatine deacons, and the suburbicarian bishops. They were the bishop of Rome's advisors and collaborators. The patriarchs, instead, are of very ancient origin and preside over their own patriarchal Churches.

The cardinals of the Holy Roman Church "assist the Roman Pontiff either collegially when they are convoked to deal with questions of major importance, or individually when they help the Roman Pontiff through the various offices they perform, especially in the daily care of the universal Church (CIC c. 349). When the Holy See is vacant, the College of Cardinals possesses only that power in the Church attributed to it in special law (CIC c. 359).

A patriarch is *father and head* of the Church over which he presides. He has power over all the bishops, including metropolitans, and other Christian faithful of his Church, according to the norm of law approved by the supreme authority (CCEO c. 56). In patriarchal Churches, the patriarchs and their synods of bishops, by ecclesiastical law, share in the supreme authority of the Church (Ap. Const. *Sacri Canones* p. XXIV).

The fact that the Eastern patriarchs who are made members of the College of Cardinals keep as their title their own patriarchal see signifies that the institution of the patriarchate is not to be linked to the historical origin of the cardinalate. Moreover, the cardinalatial dignity has the purpose of more closely and effectively associating the Eastern patriarchs with the apostolic Church of Rome and its bishop in the *sollecitudo omnium Ecclesiarum*. This universal solicitude is also expressed through the participation of the patriarchs and the hierarchs who preside over Churches *sui iuris* in the synod of bishops, which assists the Roman Pontiff in the exercise of the Petrine ministry (CCEO c. 46, §1).

Eastern Synods

Synod of Bishops

All and solely the ordained bishops of a patriarchal or major archiepiscopal Church, wherever they are constituted, must be summoned to the synod of bishops. It is for the patriarch or major archbishop to convoke the synod of bishops and to preside over it. All the bishops legitimately summoned to the synod are bound by a serious obligation to attend it, except those who have already resigned from office.

The synod of bishops of a patriarchal or major archiepiscopal Church is convoked:

- whenever business is to be transacted that pertains to the exclusive competence of the synod of bishops;
- for business the execution of which requires the consent of the synod;

- when the patriarch and the major archbishop, with the consent of the permanent synod, considers it necessary;
- when at least one- third of the members request it for a given matter, with due regard always for the rights of patriarchs, major archbishops, bishops and other persons established by common law at fixed times, even annually, if particular law so establishes it (CCEO, cc. 102-108).

The synod of bishops of a patriarchal or major archiepiscopal Church is exclusively competent to make laws for the entire patriarchal or major archiepiscopal Church that bind within the territorial boundaries of the same Church, except for liturgical laws. The synod is also the superior tribunal within the territorial boundaries of the same Church, without prejudice to the competencies of the Holy See. The synod also elects the patriarch, the major archbishop and the bishops.

The *Acta* regarding laws and decisions are to be sent to the Roman Pontiff as soon as possible; certain *acta*, or even all of them, are to be communicated to the patriarchs and major archbishops of the other Eastern Churches according to the judgment of the synod. The promulgation of laws and the publication of decisions of the synod of bishops are within the competence of the patriarch or the major archbishop (CCEO cc. 110-112).

Latin Bishops at Synod

The Eastern code c. 102, §3 foresees that "To expedite certain matters, according to the norm of particular law or with the consent of the permanent synod, others can be invited by the patriarch (or major archbishop), especially hierarchs who are not bishops and experts to give their opinions to the bishops gathered in synod." Since this canon does not make any distinctions, one can safely say that even Latin bishops who exercise their power in the same territory could be invited to the synod of bishops of a patriarchal or major archiepiscopal Church. The same norm is applicable to the council of hierarchs of the metropolitan Church *sui iuris* (CCEO c. 164, §1).

Episcopal Restrictions

Canon 102, §2 states that "With regard to eparchial bishops constituted outside the territorial boundaries of the patriarchal (and major archiepiscopal) Church and titular bishops, particular law can restrict their deliberative vote, remaining intact the canons concerning the election of the patriarch (and major archbishop), bishops and candidates for office mentioned in c. 149." A particular law excluding titular and retired bishops from deliberative vote in the election of the patriarch (and major archbishop) and bishops would be contrary to common law. Apparently the lawmaker did not establish such a law for these Eastern bishops.

Permanent Synod

The permanent synod is part of the patriarchal and major archiepiscopal curia. It is composed of the patriarch or major archbishop and four bishops designated *ad quinquennium*. Three of these bishops are elected by the synod of bishops of the patriarchal or major archiepiscopal Church; among these at least two must be eparchial bishops; the fourth bishop is appointed by the patriarch or major archbishop.

The patriarch or major archbishop convokes the permanent synod and presides over it. The permanent synod must be convoked at fixed times, at least twice a year, and whenever the patriarch or major archbishop considers it opportune, as well as whenever decisions are to be made about matters for which common law requires the consent or counsel of the permanent synod (CCEO cc. 114-116).

The consent of the permanent synod is required for certain acts of the patriarch and major archbishop, while for other acts only its view or opinion is needed. If the law requires the consent or counsel of the permanent synod for the patriarch or major archbishop to posit an act, all of its members must be convoked in accord with the norm of law (CCEO c. 948). For the juridical act to be valid, the consent of an absolute majoirity of those present is required, or the counsel of all must be sought. In cases where only counsel is required, the patriarch or major archbishop in no way is obliged to accept the synod's opinion, even if unanimous; nonetheless he is not to act contrary to that opinion, especially if unanimous, without a reason that is overriding in the patriarch's or major archbishop's judgment (CCEO c. 934). All this applies equally to the synod of bishops of the patriarchal or major archiepiscopal Church.

Election of Eastern Bishops

Within the territorial boundaries of the patriarchal or major archiepiscopal Church, bishops are designated by canonical election to a vacant eparchial see or to discharge another function, e.g., as a curial bishop. The procedure is as follows:

- Only members of the synod of the bishops of the patriarchal or major archiepiscopal Church can propose candidates suitable for the episcopate. They are to collect the information and documents that are necessary to demonstrate the suitability of the candidates. In doing so, they may, if they consider it opportune, hear in a confidential, private and individual way some presbyters and other Christian faithful outstanding in prudence and Christian life.
- The bishops are to inform the patriarch or major archbishop of their findings in a timely manner before the convocation of the syndod of bishops of the patriarchal or major archiepiscopal Church. The patriarch or major archbishop is to send this dossier, adding, if the case so suggests, further information of his own to all the members of the synod.
- The synod of bishops of the patriarchal or major archiepiscopal Church is to examine the names of the candidates and draw up by secret ballot a

list of the candidates. This list is to be transmitted through the patriarch or major archbishop to the Holy See to obtain the assent of the Roman Pontiff.

▪ Once the assent of the Roman Pontiff has been received for the individual candidates, it is valid until it is explicitly revoked, in which case the name of the candidate must be removed from the list (CCEO cc. 181-182).

The assent of the Roman Pontiff is not a mere formality; by it due consideration is given to the word of the synod and confirmed the suitability of the candidates proposed. This is an ecclesiological provision whereby the Roman Pontiff, as head of the episcopal college, knows and assents to the candidates to be incorporated into the episcopal college. The need for the Roman Pontiff's assent is based, among others, on the teaching of the Second Vatican Council: "The patriarchs of the Eastern Churches with their synods make up a higher tribunal for all matters concerning the patriarchate, including the right of setting up new eparchies and of appointing new bishops of their own rite within the confines of their own patriarchal territory, without prejudice to the inalienable right of the Roman Pontiff of intervening in individual cases [*in singulis casibus interveniendi*]" (OE 9). To accomplish this end, the Roman Pontiff avails himself of the work of the Congregation for the Eastern Churches.

Designation of Bishops Outside Patriarchal and Major Archiepiscopal Territories

As for the provisions of office of bishops – eparchial, coadjutor, auxiliary – outside the territorial boundaries of a patriarchal or major archiepiscopal Church, the synod of bishops elects, in accordance with the canons on the election of bishops, at least three candidates and proposes them through the patriarch or major archbishop to the Roman Pontiff for appointment (CCEO c. 149).

A similar procedure is prescribed for the appointment of bishops in metropolitan Churches *sui iuris* within and outside their territorial boundaries. The council of hierarchs is to compile for each case a list of at least three of the more suitable candidates and send it to the Holy See. In order to compile this list, the members of the council of hierarchs, if they consider it opportune, can seek from some presbyters or other Christian faithful who are outstanding in wisdom their opinion about the needs of the Church and the special qualities of a candidate for the episcopate (CCEO c. 168).

In Churches that are neither patriarchal, major archiepiscopal, nor metropolitan, bishops are designated by the Holy See (CCEO c. 174).

See *Assent of the Roman Pontiff to the Election of Eastern Bishops.*

Enthronement of Patriarchs and Major Archbishops

Through his enthronement a patriarch, canonically elected by the synod of bishops of the patriarchal Church, takes possession of his patriarchal see. If he accepts the election and is already an ordained bishop, the synod of bishops of the patriarchal Church proceeds according to the prescriptions of the liturgical books with his proclamation and enthronement as patriarch. If he is not yet a bishop, enthronement cannot be performed validly until he is ordained a bishop (CCEO c. 75). The patriarch, though canonically elected, validly exercises his office only after his enthronement, by which he obtains his office with the full effects of law. He is not to convoke the synod of bishops of the patriarchal Church or to ordain bishops before receiving ecclesiastical communion from the Roman Pontiff (CCEO c. 77).

As for the major archbishop of a major archiepiscopal Church, his proclamation and enthronement are to take place after the confirmation of his election by the Roman Pontiff according to CCEO cc. 63-74.

The metropolitan of a metropolitan Church *sui iuris* is appointed by the Roman Pontiff according to the norm of canon 168. Within three months of his episcopal ordination or, if already an ordained bishop, from his enthronement, he is obliged to request the pallium. Prior to the imposition of the pallium, the metropolitan cannot convoke the council of hierarchs nor ordain bishops (CCEO c. 156).

See *Eastern Patriarchs; Major Archbishops; Metropolitans of Churches Sui Iuris.*

Episcopal Vicar for Eastern Faithful

Whenever the legitimate governance of a [Latin] diocese requires it, the diocesan bishop can appoint one or more episcopal vicars, namely, those who in a specific part of the diocese or in a certain type of affairs or *over the faithful of a specific rite* or over certain groups of persons possess the same ordinary power which a vicar general has by universal law (CIC c. 476).

The Eastern code has a similar norm: "As often as the good governance of the eparchy requires it, one or several syncelli can be appointed, who have by virtue of the law itself the same authority as that which is attributed by common law to the protosyncellus but limited to a given section of the eparchy, or to certain kinds of affairs or *for the Christian faithful ascribed to another Church sui iuris* or for a certain group of persons" (CCEO c. 246).

See *Protosyncellus and Syncelli/Vicar General and Episcopal Vicars.*

Eparchy (Diocese)

Notion

The term *eparchy* derives from the Greek and is the equivalent of *diocese* in Latin law. As is well-known, the Roman Empire was divided into four *Prefectures,* which were in turn subdivided into *Dioceses, Eparchies,* and *Parishes.* Emperor Diocletian, circa 297, divided his empire into twelve Dioceses, which were subdivided into several provinces, called eparchies. In ecclesiastical terminology, the West chose the term *diocese* and the East the term *eparchy* to indicate the ecclesiastical territorial division of the local Church entrusted to the governance of a bishop.

In today's Eastern law an eparchy is a portion of the people of God that is entrusted to a bishop to shepherd, with the cooperation of the presbyters, in such a way that, adhering to its pastor and gathered by him through the Gospel and the Eucharist in the Holy Spirit, it constitutes a particular Church in which the one, holy, catholic and apostolic Church of Christ truly exists and is operative (CCEO c. 177, §1). The bishop who governs an eparchy is called the *eparchial bishop*. He is frequently called *eparch*, but this term does not appear in the current Eastern code.

The code states: "The eparchial bishop, to whom the eparchy has been entrusted to shepherd in his own name, governs it as the vicar and legate of Christ; the power which he exercises personally in the name of Christ, is proper, ordinary, and immediate, although by the supreme authority of the Church its exercise is ultimately regulated and can be circumscribed within certain limits in view of the benefit of the Church or the Christian faithful" (CCEO c. 178).

Exarchy (Vicariate)

An exarchy is a portion of the people of God which, because of special circumstances, is not erected as an eparchy, and which, being delimited territorially or by some other criterion, is entrusted to an exarch to shepherd (CCEO c. 311, §1). The exarch governs the exarchy either in the name of the one who appointed him (Patriarch or Roman Pontiff), or in his own name. This must be established in the erection or modification of the exarchy (CCEO c. 312). Within the boundaries of the territory of the patriarchal or major archiepiscopal Church, the patriarch or the major archbishop, with the consent of the permanent synod, can erect, modify and suppress exarchies (CCEO c. 85, §3).

Apostolic exarchies are equivalent to the apostolic vicariates of the Latin Church; they are ecclesiastical territorial divisions entrusted to exarchs and established in territories not subject to a patriarch or major archbishop. Outside the boundaries of the territory of a patriarchal Church, an exarchy is erected by the Holy See (CCEO c. 311, §2), and its exarch is appointed by the Roman Pontiff.

Patriarchal, major archiepiscopal and apostolic exarchs are usually bishops and, since they do not have residential sees, titular episcopal sees are conferred on them.

An exarch constituted outside the territorial boundaries of the patriarchal Church can ask the patriarch for suitable presbyters to see to the pastoral care of the Christian faithful. The patriarch is to satisfy this request, as far as possible. The presbyters sent to an exarchy by the patriarch, either for a determined or indeterminate time, are considered attached to the exarchy and are subject in all things to the power of the exarch (CCEO c. 315).

Latin Metropolitans and Eastern Bishops in the Diaspora

The Eastern code c. 139 requires that the eparchial bishop who exercises his power outside the territorial boundaries of the patriarchal Church and does not belong to a province must designate a particular Metropolitan, having consulted with the patriarch and with the approval of the Holy See; to this metropolitan belong the rights and obligations set forth in c. 133 §1, 3°-6°.

Obviously, in Latin territories this Metropolitan could even be a Latin who, in regard to the extra-territorial Eastern eparchy, has the following functions:

- to erect the Metropolitan tribunal;
- to be vigilant that the faith and ecclesiastical discipline be accurately observed;
- to conduct a canonical visitation, if the eparchial bishop neglected to do so;
- to appoint or confirm a person who has been legitimately proposed for or elected to an office, if the eparchial bishop, even though not prevented by a just impediment, has failed to do so within the time established by law;
- to appoint the eparchial finance officer if the eparchial bishop, though warned, has neglected to do so.

As one can see, these are the same rights and duties of that a Latin Metropolitan exercises over his ecclesiastical province (CIC cc. 436; 1438). Latin metropolitans can also receive additional special faculties and powers from the Holy See in regard to the Eastern eparchies.

Major Archbishop

A major archbishop is the metropolitan of a see determined or recognized by the supreme authority of the Church, who presides over an entire Eastern Church *sui iuris* that is not endowed with a patriarchal title. What is stated in common law concerning patriarchal Churches or patriarchs is understood to be applicable equally to major archiepiscopal Churches and major archbishops, unless common law expressly provides otherwise or it is evident from the nature of the matter.

A major archbishop is elected by the synod of the bishops of the major archiepiscopal Church, constituted within and outside the territory of the Church. After the person elected has accepted the election, the synod must inform the Roman Pontiff in writing about the canonical conduct of the election. In addition, the elected person must, in a letter written in his own hand, petition the Roman Pontiff for confirmation of his election.

After the confirmation has been obtained, the person elected must, in the presence of the synod, make a profession of faith and promise to fulfill his office faithfully; this is followed by his proclamation and enthronement. If, however, the one who is elected is not yet ordained a bishop, the enthronement cannot take place validly until he receives episcopal ordination. If confirmation of the election were to be denied, a new election is to be conducted within the time established by the Roman Pontiff.

Major archbishops have precedence of honor immediately after patriarchs, according to the order in which their Church was erected as a major archiepiscopal Church (CCEO cc. 151-154; OE 10). Currently, there are four major archiepiscopal Catholic Churches: Ukrainian, Syro-Malabar, Syro-Malankara, and Romanian.

See *Competence of the Patriarch on Canonical Provisions in His Territory.*

Metropolitans of Churches *Sui Iuris*

A Metropolitan is an eparchial bishop who presides over a Church *sui iuris*. Currently, there are three Metropolitan Churches *sui iuris*: the Ethiopian Church of Addis Ababa, the Ruthenian Church of Pittsburgh, and the Slovak Church of Prešov. The power that a Metropolitan possesses in accord with the norm of law over the bishops, clergy and other Christian faithful of his Metropolitan Church is ordinary and proper, but personal (CCEO cc. 155; 157). According to ancient tradition, he is by his office and prerogatives the true "ritual head" of the Metropolitan Church *sui iuris* over which he presides. Therefore, his role differs significantly from that of Latin Metropolitans and Metropolitans of patriarchal and major archiepiscopal Churches. The rights and obligations of the latter two are established by the competent authority (CCEO cc. 133; 138).

The nomination of the Metropolitan of a Metropolitan Church *sui iuris* is reserved to the Roman Pontiff. The Council of Hierarchs compiles for each case a list of at least three of the more suitable candidates and sends it to the Holy See, observing confidentiality even with the candidates (CCEO c. 168). The newly-enthroned Metropolitan is bound by the obligation to request from the Roman Pontiff the pallium, a symbol of metropolitan power and of the full communion of the metropolitan Church *sui iuris* with the successor of Peter (CCEO c. 156).

In his Metropolitan Church *sui iuris*, besides that which is accorded him by common law or particular law established by the Roman Pontiff, the Metropolitan is competent:

- to ordain and enthrone bishops of the same Church;
- to convoke the Council of Hierarchs, to prepare an agenda to be treated in it, to preside, transfer, prorogue, suspend or dissolve it;
- to erect the Metropolitan tribunal;
- to exercise vigilance so that faith and ecclesiastical discipline are accurately observed;
- to conduct a canonical visitation if the eparchial bishop has neglected to do so;
- to appoint an administrator of a vacant eparchy if within eight days the administrator has not been elected or if the one elected lacks the required qualities;

- to appoint or confirm a person who has been legitimately proposed for or elected to an office if the eparchial bishop, though not prevented by a just impediment, has failed to do so;
- to appoint the eparchial finance officer if the eparchial bishop, though warned, has neglected to make the appointment;
- to communicate the acts of the Roman Pontiff to the eparchial bishops and others concerned, unless the Holy See has directly provided for it, and see to the faithful execution of the prescriptions contained in the acts (CCEO c. 159).

The Metropolitan represents the Metropolitan Church *sui iuris* in all its juridic affairs (CCEO c. 157, §3). According to canonical directives (CCEO cc. 163; 208, §2) and the praxis of the Roman curia, the Metropolitan, together with all the bishops of the Metropolitan Church, must make the visit *ad limina apostolorum* every five years.

See *Council of Hierarchs of a Metropolitan Church Sui Iuris.*

Territorial Power of Eastern Hierarchs

Norm

The Eastern code c. 78, §2 states: "The power of the patriarch is exercised validly only within the territorial boundaries of the patriarchal Church unless the nature of the matter or the common or particular law approved by the Roman Pontiff establishes otherwise." Canon 147 also states that the power of the patriarch and the synod is exercised within the territorial boundaries of the patriarchal Church.

This norm, which also applies to major archiepiscopal and metropolitan *sui iuris* Churches (CCEO cc. 152 & 157), upholds the general principle already established by the first ecumenical councils and the Decree on the Eastern Churches (*Orientalium Ecclesiarum*) on the territoriality of the power of the Eastern ecclesiastical authorities. Consequently, the principle of the non-extension (*principio della non-estensione*) of this power over the faithful of their own Church *sui iuris* residing outside the territorial boundaries is herein confirmed.

However, for the Eastern Churches, in special situations in which their faithful reside outside the territory of origin, the synods of bishops of the various Churches should develop detailed proposals that are clearly based on the code, when it is deemed opportune to draft a *ius speciale ad tempus* to be approved by the Roman Pontiff. The common law does not allow Eastern authorities to erect eparchies and exarchies outside of their territories, no less designate bishops for them (CCEO cc. 177, §2; 311, §2; 181; 149).

Ius Vigilantiae (The Right of Vigilance)

It is the right and the obligation of the patriarch or major archbishop to seek appropriate information concerning the Christian faithful who reside outside of the territorial boundaries of the Church over which he presides, even through a visitor sent by him with the assent of the Holy See. The visitor, having completed the visitation, is to submit a report to the patriarch or major archbishop, who, after discussing the matter in the synod of bishops, can propose suitable measures to the Holy See; the purpose of such proposals is to provide for the protection and enhancement throughout the world of the spiritual good of the Eastern Christian faithful, even by erecting parishes and exarchies or eparchies of their own (CCEO c.153).

Patriarch's Faculties Outside His Territory

The patriarch has the faculty to ordain and enthrone metropolitans and other bishops of his patriarchal Church constituted outside of the territorial boundaries of his Church (CCEO c. 86, §2). Before their episcopal ordination, these candidates are to make the profession of faith and promise of obedience to the patriarch in matters in which they are subject to him in accord with the norm of law (CCEO c. 187, §2).

These same hierarchs are required to send a copy of the quinquennial report to their patriarch (CCEO cc. 206, §2; 318, §2). The eparchial bishop who exercises power outside of the territorial boundaries of the patriarchal Church and does not belong to a province is to consult the patriarch before designating a certain metropolitan (CCEO c. 139).

The patriarch can send suitable presbyters, upon request of the exarchs, to undertake the pastoral care of the Christian faithful residing outside of the territorial boundaries of the patriarchal Church (CCEO c. 315).

In places where not even an exarchy has been erected for the Christian faithful of a certain patriarchal Church, the patriarch, with the assent of the Holy See, can designate for them a bishop of another Church *sui iuris*, even of the Latin Church, who is to be considered their proper hierarch (CCEO c. 916, §5). As a rule, there is only one bishop who, in accordance with the norm of law, is the ordinary of the place in which these Eastern faithful reside.

The patriarch is to be contacted by bishops who wish to appoint presbyters, pastors or syncelli for the care of the Christian faithful of the patriarchal Church. If the patriarch should disagree for whatever reason, the matter is to be referred to the Holy See (CCEO c. 193, §3).

The patriarch is endowed by law with the personal faculty to bless marriages everywhere, as long as at least one of the parties is ascribed to the Church over which he presides (CCEO c. 829, §3). These faculties are also applicable to major archbishops.

CANONICAL ISSUES

Application of the Two Codes and their Inter-relations

Recipients of the Two Codes

The very first canon of the Latin and Eastern codes establishes their passive subjects and the criteria governing mutual relations, that is, the personal limits of their effectiveness. This takes place in two different ways:

The Latin code binds only the Latin Church, making no reference to the Eastern faithful; the Eastern code, on the other hand, makes some exceptions, which must be expressly established (*expresse*, that is, *explicite* or *implicite*).

In the Eastern code, canon 1 states that, "the canons of this code concern all and only the Eastern Catholic Churches, unless, with regard to relations with the Latin Church, it is expressly established otherwise (*aliud expresse statuitur*)." The equivalent canon of the Latin code states simply that "the canons of this code regard only the Latin Church." It is therefore very clear that the Eastern code binds exclusively the members of all the Eastern Catholic Churches. In other words, the limits of application of the legislative norms are all and only the Eastern Catholic Churches *sui iuris*.

Taking into account the equivalent Latin canon, one can surmise that the basis in both codes is postulated by the application of one of the fundamental principles of legal logic according to which each code, as every law or legal norm, must clearly specify its proper subjects.

CCEO Norms Regarding Latin Catholics

The Eastern code contains norms that expressly pertain to the Latin Church and, therefore, also directly bind the Latin faithful. In fact, the Latin Church is explicitly mentioned by the formula *etiam Ecclesia Latina* in nine canons: 37; 41; 207; 322, §1; 432; 696; 830, §1; 916, §5; 1465. By inserting the phrase *etiam Ecclesia Latina*, the Eastern code in dealing with Christian faithful and ministers of any Church *sui iuris* intends to include the Latin Church. With the phrase "unless it is expressly established otherwise" (*nisi aliud expresse statuitur*) the legislator refers not only to the explicit norms of the code, but also to other norms and principles contained in it which, from the nature of the matter dealt with, or from the mind of the legislator, or from the purpose of the norm, pertain to all the Christian faithful, both Eastern and Latin. There are other canons in which, while the Latin Church is not expressly named, it is still included as a Church *sui iuris*, though differing from the four types of Churches *sui iuris* listed in the Eastern code.

In Title II, the Eastern code deals with the Latin Church, either in its single members or in its collectivity, regarding ascription to a Church *sui iuris* and observance of rites. Several canons demand a certain unity of action among the bishops who exercise their power in the same territory, without any regard to rite, and therefore also bind the Latin Church. This is also true for general ecclesiastical discipline: to foster more harmoniously the unity of all Christians (CCEO c. 84, §1); to see that, after mutual consultation, the same norm is established regarding fees and offerings (c. 1013, §2); to have penal laws that are uniform in the same territory (c. 1405, §3). The superiors of religious institutes of the Latin Church that accept Eastern candidates must also observe cc. 451 and 517, §2 of the Eastern code.

Indirectly these canons bind even the Latin Church, especially the ecclesiastical authorities who have power over Eastern faithful (CCEO c. 916, §5). It suffices here to mention norms that determine the juridical condition of physical persons within the ecclesiastical community, recognizing or denying their suitability to posit certain acts -- for example, minor or major age, or their free state. These laws ought to be observed by any ecclesiastical superior, whether Eastern or Latin.

CIC Norms Regarding Eastern Catholics

The principle contained in the first canon of the Eastern code applies also to the equivalent canon of the Latin code which states that "the canons of this code regard only the Latin Church ... unless, with regard to relations with the Eastern Churches, they expressly establish otherwise." In fact, the Latin code includes a number of norms that directly bind Eastern Catholics (cc. 111, §1; 112, §2; 214; 372, §2; 383, §2; 450, §1, 476; 479, §2; 518; 535, §2; 846, §2; 923; 991; 1015, §2; 1021; 1109; 1248, §1). With this parallel codification (CCEO c. 1 and CIC c. 1), one can assert that every Eastern Catholic is subject to the common law of the universal Catholic Church, the common law of the Eastern Catholic Churches, and the particular law of the Eastern Church *sui iuris,* to which he or she is ascribed, and every Latin Catholic is equally subject to the common law of the universal Catholic Church, the common law of the Latin Church, and the personal or territorial particular law (CIC cc. 12-13).

Autonomy of the Two Codes

Even though the two codes are independent, their respective General Norms are applicable to cases in which the canons of the Eastern code may be able to resolve doubts or to clarify ambiguity present in parallel canons of the Latin code. This does not mean that the Eastern code should be viewed as a supplement or source of law for the Latin code, or the Latin code as a supplement or source of law for the Eastern code. Canonical science indicates that one code can make up for the other only as a guide, not as a precept. Both codes, however, follow the same principle of legal interpretation: "Laws must be understood according to the proper meaning of the words considered in their text and context. If the meaning remains doubtful and obscure, they must be understood according to parallel passages, if there are such, to the purpose and circumstances of the law, and to the mind of the legislator" (CCEO c. 1499; CIC c.17).

See *Common and Particular Eastern Law.*

Common and Particular Eastern Law

Preliminaries

In the Eastern code the phrase *common law* includes, besides the laws and legitimate customs of the entire Church, the laws and legitimate customs common to all the Eastern Churches. The phrase *particular law* includes all laws, legitimate customs, statutes and other norms of law, that are neither common to the entire Church nor to all the Eastern Churches (CCEO c. 1493), but only to the individual Churches *sui iuris.* Also particular law encompasses the laws and decrees enacted by eparchial bishops, the statutes and constitutions (*typica*) of monasteries and religious institutes, the liturgical laws and prescriptions of the Churches *sui iuris*, the agreements and personal statutes stipulated by the Churches *sui iuris* and the civil authorities (CCEO cc. 98 & 99)

In a broad sense, *Eastern canon law* means the canonical discipline that regulates the life of all and only the Eastern Catholic Churches. Historically it originated from the ecumenical councils, local synods, Roman pontiffs and dicasteries, and from the legislative bodies of the Eastern Churches. Currently, the canonical discipline common to all the Eastern Catholic Churches is contained mainly in the *Codex Canonum Ecclesiarum Orientalium* (CCEO) promulgated by Pope John Paul II on October 18, 1990, effective October 1, 1991. The individual Eastern Churches *sui iuris* have the right to govern themselves according to their own special disciplines (OE 5), that is, their particular rights and privileges that have been in use and never revoked.

Sources of Eastern Law

The sources of law common to the Eastern Churches are first of all the *sacri canones*, that is, the ancient law received or adapted to the needs of the times. These canons were put forth by the divine Apostles, as tradition has it, and by "the six holy and universal synods and local councils" as well as "by our holy Fathers." (John Paul II, Apostolic Constitution *Sacri Canones*). These canons of the first centuries have been ratified by the Fathers of the Councils of Constantinople in 691 (canon 2) and Nicea in 787 (canon 1).

Other sources of law in force common to the Eastern Catholic Churches are the Acts of the Roman Pontiffs and the Holy See enacted since the time of their union with Rome. The Second Vatican Council promulgated a special decree on the Eastern Catholic Churches, *Orientalium Ecclesiarum*, which contains certain disciplinary norms and some principles of revision for the Eastern law. Before Vatican II parts of the common Eastern law were promulgated in the years 1949-1957 by Pope Pius XII as *motu proprio* – *Crebrae allatae*, on marriage; *Sollicitudinem nostram*, on trials and processes; *Postquam apostolicis litteris*, on religious and temporal goods; *Cleri sanctitati*, on rites and persons.

Firmness of Canon Law (CCEO & CIC)

The norms of the *Code of Canons of the Eastern Churches* (CCEO) have the same firmness, strength and stability as the norms of the *Code of Canon Law* (CIC) of the Latin Church, that is, they remain in force until abrogated or changed by the supreme authority of the Church for just reasons. The most serious of those reasons is the full communion of all the Eastern Churches with the Catholic Church. The simple fact that the Catholic Church embraces in its canonical order one Eastern law and one Latin law demonstrates very clearly the universality of the Church, which is gathered by the one Spirit and, as it were, breathes with the two lungs of the East and West, and burns in the love of Christ, having one heart, as it were, with two ventricles (Pope John Paul II).

Enactment of Laws

Liturgical Norms

Patriarchal Churches are competent to issue liturgical norms that, enacted by the synod of bishops of the patriarchal Church and promulgated by the patriarch, obtain the force of law everywhere in the world (CCEO c. 150, §2). This is also applicable to major archiepiscopal Churches and major archbishops (CCEO c. 152). The council of hierarchs of a metropolitan Church *sui iuris* can enact laws and norms in cases in which common law remits the matter to the particular law of a Church *sui iuris* (CCEO cc. 167, §1-3; 169). In all Churches *sui iuris* that are neither patriarchal, major archiepiscopal nor metropolitan, the hierarchs who preside over them are appointed by the Holy See. These hierarchs are the competent authority in their Churches to enact particular norms in accordance with the norm of law and the consent of the Holy See (CCEO cc. 174-176).

Disciplinary Laws

Disciplinary laws and other decisions enacted by the synod of bishops of the patriarchal Church and promulgated by the patriarch have the force of law within the territorial boundaries of the patriarchal Church. This provision is also applicable to major archiepiscopal Churches and metropolitan Churches *sui iuris*. Eparchial bishops constituted outside of the territorial boundaries of the patriarchal Church who desire to do so can attribute the force of law in their own eparchies to such disciplinary laws and other synodal decisions, provided that they do not exceed their competence. Of course, if these laws or decisions are approved by the Holy See, they have the force of law everywhere in the world (CCEO c. 150, §§2-3).

Minors and their Juridical Status

Catholic Father and Christian Mother: A son or daughter who has not yet completed fourteen years of age is ascribed by virtue of baptism to the Church *sui iuris* to which his or her Catholic father is ascribed (CCEO c. 29, §1).

Catholic Mother and Christian Father: A son or daughter who has not yet completed fourteen years is ascribed by virtue of baptism to the Church *sui iuris* to which his or her Catholic mother is ascribed (CCEO c. 29, §1).

Catholic Father and Non-Baptized Mother: A son or daughter who has not yet completed fourteen years of age is ascribed by virtue of baptism to the Church *sui iuris* to which his or her Catholic father is ascribed (CCEO c. 29, §1).

Catholic Mother and Non-Baptized Father: A son or daughter who has not yet completed fourteen years of age is ascribed by virtue of baptism to the Church *sui iuris* to which his or her Catholic mother is ascribed (CCEO c. 29, §1).

Unwed Catholic Mother: A son or daughter of an unwed mother who has not yet completed fourteen years of age is ascribed by virtue of baptism to the Church *sui iuris* to which his or her mother is ascribed (CCEO c. 29, §2, 1°).

Unknown Parents: A son or daughter of unknown parents who has not yet completed fourteen years of age is ascribed by virtue of baptism to the Church *sui iuris* to which belong those to whose care he or she has been legitimately entrusted (CCEO c. 29, §2, 2°).

Adoptive Parents: A son or daughter of adoptive parents who has not yet completed fourteen years of age is ascribed by virtue of baptism to the Church *sui iuris* to which the Catholic adoptive parents belong (CCEO c. 29, §2, 2°; §1).

Non-Baptized Parents: A son or daughter of non-baptized parents who has not yet completed fourteen years of age is ascribed by virtue of baptism to the Church *sui iuris* to which belongs the one who has assumed his or her education in the Catholic faith (CCEO c. 29, §2, 3°).

Orthodox Parents: Infants of non-Catholic Christians are licitly baptized if their parents – or at least one of them or the person who legitimately takes their place – request it and if it physically or morally impossible for them to approach their own minister (CCEO c. 681, §5). Note that the Latin code does not have an equivalent norm; this *lacuna legis* should be resolved in light of the Eastern norm (CIC c. 19).

In this case, a minor son or daughter of Orthodox, baptized by necessity in the Latin Church or in an Eastern Catholic Church, belongs to the Orthodox Church of the parents. If the Orthodox parents, however, at the celebration of baptism or afterwards, expressly request the reception of their minor son or daughter into the Catholic Church, their child is ascribed to the Church of the same rite as the parents on condition that "there is a founded hope that the minor will be educated in the Catholic Church" (CCEO cc. 900; 681, §1, 1°; CIC c. 868, §1, 2°).

Perhaps a more debated issue among canon lawyers is the juridical state of a minor born of a Catholic-Orthodox marriage and baptized in the Orthodox Church. Canon 29, §1 of the Eastern code explicitly refers to the case of a Catholic father or mother in a mixed marriage and states that the son or daughter who has not yet completed the fourteenth year of age is ascribed in virtue of baptism to the Church *sui iuris* to which the Catholic parent is ascribed.

Canon 112, §1, 3° of the Latin code regulates the case of the Catholic party who, in a mixed marriage, legitimately transfers to another ritual Church. In this situation, the son or daughter who has not yet completed the fourteenth year of age also transfers to the ritual Church of the Catholic parent.

This problem is present in many countries, especially in the Middle East, where mixed marriages are customary, and the baptism of the children has canonical, ecumenical, social and civil implications. In fact, these children, in virtue of their baptism, are ascribed to the Church to which the father, Catholic or Orthodox, is ascribed.

In the new Latin and Eastern legislation the determining factor for ascription to a Church *sui iuris* is not the liturgical rite in which a person is baptized but the parents' membership in a specific Church *sui iuris*. The liturgical rite in which a person is baptized does not entail his or her automatic ascription to the same Church: the liturgical rite of baptism must correspond to the rite of the Church *sui iuris* to which the person-to-be-baptized is to be ascribed, not vice versa.

If a person, for legitimate or illegitimate reasons, is baptized according to the liturgical rite of a Church *sui iuris* different from the one to which his or her parents are ascribed, this does not entail ascription to the Church of baptism. According to this principle, the prevailing praxis followed by the Congregation for the Eastern Churches seems clear: children of mixed marriages, independently of their baptism in the Orthodox Church, are members of the Catholic Church. This praxis corresponds to the Church's obligation to safeguard the Catholic faith of these children.

Personal Statutes

The preliminary canons of the Eastern code deal, among other things, with "agreements entered into or approved by the Holy See with nations or other political societies" (CCEO c. 4). By adding the phrase "or approved" the lawmaker opens the door to the possibility that others may draw up an agreement with a civil authority, as foreseen in c. 98 for the patriarch who presides over his patriarchal Church. In fact, besides the Holy See, the patriarch, too, "with the consent of the synod of bishops of the patriarchal Church and the prior assent of the Roman Pontiff, can enter into agreements with a civil authority that are not contrary to the law established by the Holy See; the patriarch cannot put these same agreements into effect without having obtained the approval of the Roman Pontiff." These agreements, in as much as they have been approved by the Holy See, remain in effect, as they have been up to the present time, in accord with CCEO c. 4, notwithstanding contrary prescriptions.

This canon allows the term "agreements" (*conventiones*) to be interpreted in a broad, rather than a narrow, sense, that is, the patriarch can simultaneously enter into agreements with various civil authorities in whose territories the patriarchal Church is present. The term "agreements" therefore can include a treaty as understood by public ecclesiastical law or concordatory law, or a treaty of international public law. "Agreement" very often indicates an international accord of a less solemn form, not subject to solemn ratification, but signed by governmental representatives. The patriarch is to see that, in regions where these agreements (personal statutes) are in force, they are observed by everyone. If several patriarchs in the same area exercise powers recognized or conceded in the personal statutes, it is expedient that, in matters of greater importance (*in negotiis maioris momenti*), they act only after consulting one another.

"Personal statutes" means a law enacted by a civil legislator for the benefit of a particular religious community by which certain rights are accorded to that community. This has its origin in the concession by Muslim rulers of certain autonomy and powers to patriarchs of the Eastern Churches in the Middle Ages so that their Christian subjects could be treated as a separate community, or *millet*, ruled by its own religious leaders. Today, this provision has been accorded to various religious communities by secular civil governments. Undoubtedly, "Civil law, to which the law of the Church yields, is to be observed in the canon law with the same effects, insofar as they are not contrary to divine law and unless canon law provides otherwise" (CCEO c. 1504).

The patriarch, endowed with the required powers of concordatory law, can reserve to himself matters that concern several eparchies and affect the civil authorities; he cannot, however, decide on such matters without consulting the eparchial bishops concerned and without the consent of the permanent synod. If the matter is urgent and time is too short to convene the bishop-members of the permanent synod, the bishops of the eparchial curia or the two eparchial bishops who are senior by episcopal ordination may substitute for them (CCEO c. 100). The same also applies to major archbishops (CCEO c. 152).

Note that, although the qualified party (*subjectum habile*) to enter into agreements is the Holy See, the phrase "entered into or approved by the Holy See" in CCEO c. 4 clearly implies that lower authorities can also enter into agreements that will later on be approved by the Holy See. The Latin code does not contain a similar provision (CIC c. 3), but *de facto* the conferences of bishops deal with civil authorities on matters of common interest.

Resignation from Office

Patriarchs or Major Archbishops
The Eastern code does not set any age limit for resignation from office of a patriarch or major archbishop. Therefore, particular law cannot establish any limit for such resignation, unless the requirements for one to be considered a candidate for the patriarchal or major archiepiscopal dignity specify that one who has completed a determined age cannot be elected (CCEO c. 64).

The synod of bishops is competent to accept the resignation of the patriarch or major archbishop, after having consulted with the Roman Pontiff, unless the patriarch or major archbishop approaches the Pope directly (CCEO c. 126, §2).

The resigned patriarch or major archbishop retains his title and honors, especially in liturgical celebrations, and has the right to be assigned a dignified residence that meets with his approval and is to be provided with resources, drawn from the goods of the Church, to provide for a dignified support corresponding to his title (CCEO c. 62).

Bishops
An eparchial bishop who has completed his seventy-fifth year of age or who, because of ill health or some other serious reason, has become less able to fulfill his office, is requested (*rogatur*) to resign from office. This resignation is to be presented to the patriarch or major archbishop in the case

of an eparchial bishop exercising authority within the territorial boundaries of the patriarchal or major archiepiscopal Church; in other cases, it is presented to the Roman Pontiff.

To accept this resignation, the patriarch or major archbishop needs the consent of the permanent synod, unless a request (invitation) for resignation was made previously by the synod of bishops of the patriarchal or major archiepiscopal Church" (CCEO c. 210, §3). The eparchial bishop, whose resignation from office has been accepted, obtains the title of 'eparchial bishop emeritus' of the eparchy he governed (CCEO c. 211, §1). Coadjutor bishops or auxiliary bishops who resign from office are given the title of "emeritus" of the office they previously carried out (CCEO c. 218).

The synod of bishops of the patriarchal or major archiepiscopal Church or the council of hierarchs must see that provision is made for the suitable and dignified support of the bishop emeritus, with due regard for the primary obligation, which rests with the eparchy he served (CCEO c. 211).

Pastors

Pastors cease from office by resignation accepted by the eparchial bishop, expiration of a determined term, removal, or transfer. When pastors have completed their seventy-fifth year of age, they are requested to submit their resignation from office to the eparchial bishop, who, after considering all circumstances of person and place, is to decide whether to accept or defer the resignation; the eparchial bishop, taking into account the norms of particular law is to provide for the suitable support and residence of the resigned pastors (CCEO c. 297).

Superiors of Monasteries

The office of superior of a monastery *sui iuris* is conferred for an indeterminate time, unless the typicon or statutes determines otherwise. This provision reflects the ancient tradition but also allows some adaptation for a determinate time of office. Nonetheless, superiors who have completed the seventy-fifth year of age or who have become unfit to fulfill their office because of failing health or another grave cause, are to present their resignation from office to the synaxis; it is for the synaxis to accept it (CCEO c. 444).

The superiors of religious orders and congregations are to be constituted for a determined and appropriate period of time, unless the statutes establish otherwise for the superior general (CCEO c. 514, §1).

EASTERN CHURCHES

Congregation for the Eastern Churches

The origin of this dicastery dates back to the Congregation *de Propaganda Fide* for the Affairs of the Oriental Rite established by Pope Pius IX on January 6, 1862, with the apostolic constitution *Romani Pontifices*. On May 1,

1917, Pope Benedict XV with the motu proprio *Dei Providentis* made this an independent dicastery entitled Congregation for the Oriental Church. Its competence was greatly widened by Pope Pius XI with the motu proprio *Sancta Dei Ecclesia* on March 25, 1938. Pope Paul VI with the apostolic constitution *Regimini Ecclesiae Universae* on August 15, 1967, modified the name to Congregation for the Eastern Churches, reflecting the variety of the Eastern Catholic Churches, which today number twenty-one.

The Congregation is presided over by a Prefect, assisted by a Secretary and an Under-Secretary. Members of this dicastery are the cardinals appointed by the Roman pontiff and *ex officio* the patriarchs of the Eastern Catholic Churches, the major archbishops, and the President of the Pontifical Council for Promoting Christian Unity. Among its collaborators the Congregation includes various officials who address the day-to-day needs of the Churches, numerous consultors, and other employees.

According to the apostolic constitution *Pastor Bonus* of Pope John Paul II, promulgated on June 28, 1988, the competence of this congregation extends to all matters that are proper to the Eastern Churches and are to be referred to the Holy See – the structure and organization of the Churches, the exercise of the office of teaching, sanctifying and governing, and the status, rights, and obligations of persons. It also handles everything that has to be done concerning quinquennial reports, the *ad limina* visits (CCEO cc. 92, §3; 134, §2; 208, §§1-2; 317), and inter-ritual affairs such as the transfer to another Church *sui iuris* (CCEO c. 32; CIC c. 112, §1, 1°).

The Congregation for the Eastern Churches exercises *ad normam iuris* for the Eastern eparchies, hierarchs, clergy, monastics, religious and lay faithful the same faculties that the Congregations for Bishops, for the Clergy, for Institutes of Consecrated Life and Societies of Apostolic Life, and for Divine Worship and the Discipline of the Sacraments exercise for Latin dioceses, bishops, clergy, monks, nuns, religious, and lay faithful. It has also authority over Eastern and Latin persons residing in "Eastern regions," that is, Egypt and the Sinai Peninsula, Eritrea, Ethiopia, South Albania, Bulgaria, Cyprus, Greece, Iran, Iraq, Lebanon, Palestine, Syria, Jordan, and Turkey.

Currently, the Vatican Secretariate of State (the Section for Relations with States) is competent – *donec aliter provideatur* – for the constitution, provision and alteration of jurisdiction over the Eastern and Latin institutions in Albania, Armenia, Azerbaijan, Bielorussia, Bosnia-Herzegovina, Georgia, Kazakhstan, Kyrgyzstan, Macedonia, Moldovia, Montenegro, Russia, Serbia, Tadjikistan, Turkmenistan, Ukraine and Uzbekistan, which proceeds in consultation with (*collatis consiliis*) either the Congregation for the Eastern Churches or the Congregation for Bishops or the Congregation for the Evangelization of Peoples.

On the other hand, the Congregations for the Doctrine of the Faith and for the Causes of Saints, and the Tribunals of the Apostolic Penitentiary, the Apostolic Signatura, and the Roman Rota, all have competence over the entire Catholic Church, with the exclusion of the Congregation for the Eastern Churches.

Moreover, the Congregation for Divine Worship and the Discipline of the Sacraments is competent for the *ratum et non consummatum* marriage cases; the Congregation for the Clergy handles dispensations from Holy Orders; and the Congregation for Catholic Education exercises jurisdiction over Catholic universities and faculties, including Eastern institutions.

See *Faculties/Competence of the Congregation for the Eastern Churches.*

Eastern Churches *Sui Iuris*

Notion and Juridical State in the Universal Church

The term *Ecclesia sui iuris* in the Eastern code means a self-ruling Church, a Church with its own specific discipline, a Church that is regulated by its own internal statutes. It is imprecise to call an *Ecclesia sui iuris* an "autonomous Church" or an "autocephalous Church" or an "individual Church."

The constitutive elements of a Church *sui iuris* are set forth in the CCEO c. 27:

1. A community of the Christian faithful -- that is, an ecclesial assembly of *Christifideles*: faithful, clerics, monastics and religious.
2. Joined together by a hierarchy according to the norm of the law -- that is, a proper hierarchy legitimately constituted in compliance with canon law. This hierarchy unites these *Christifideles* in one particular ecclesial community and organizes them into a homogeneous grouping as one Church. The proper hierarchy is an organic element of cohesion and unity, a guarantee of the ecclesial communion.
3. And which is expressly or tacitly recognized as *sui iuris* by the supreme authority: the express or tacit recognition by the supreme authority of a particular Church thus composed and organized with a proper hierarchy is essential. Hierarchical communion with the Roman Pontiff, understood as unity and organic reality, is a constitutive element of the canonical status of the *Ecclesia sui iuris*. It is this hierarchical communion with the Apostolic See of Rome that guarantees the ecclesiological and canonical status of the Eastern Catholic Churches *sui iuris*.

The first two elements – community of faithful and hierarchy – are significant inner elements, but they are not sufficient without the third external, formal element, that is, recognition of the aforesaid self-rule by the supreme authority of the Church.

Relative Self-rule of the Eastern Churches Sui Iuris

The express or tacit recognition by the supreme authority of the Church as an external element and essential criterion for the legal status of a Church *sui iuris* means that its self-rule is relative, defined by the norm of law promulgated or approved by the supreme authority of the Church. It is up to the supreme authority of the Church to recognize an individual single community as a "Church *sui iuris*" and also to determine in canonical norms the limit of its self-rule, without prejudice to the right to intervene in special cases.

The self-rule of the Churches *sui iuris* is put into effect by the Vatican II provision of "governing themselves in accordance with their own particular rules" (OE 5), deriving from the common law (c. 1493, §1), the particular law (c. 1493, §2), and exercising justice appropriately so that the ecclesial community lives peacefully and pursues its proper goals. Whereas individual hierarchs care for their own eparchies, the heads of the Churches *sui iuris* – patriarchs, major archbishops and metropolitans – enjoy a higher authority over their respective Churches. Canon 27, limiting itself to the strictly legal concept of *Ecclesia sui iuris*, does not include the element of *Ritus* in this definition.

Typology of the Eastern Churches Sui Iuris

The Eastern code, dealing with the various Eastern Churches *sui iuris*, makes specific reference to the Eastern Catholic Churches:

- the Patriarchal Churches: Coptic, Syriac, Maronite, Melkite, Chaldean and Armenian (cc. 55-150);
- the Major Archiepiscopal Churches: Ukrainian, Syro-Malabar, Syro-Malankara and Rumenian, which, with some exceptions, are similar to the patriarchal ones (cc.151-154);
- the Metropolitan Churches: Ethiopian, Ruthenian, and Slovak (cc. 155-173);
- other Churches *sui iuris* (entrusted to a hierarch who presides over it according to the norm of common law and the particular law established by the Roman Pontiff): Albanian, Bielorussian, Bulgarian, Crisiensis (Križevci), Hellenic, Hungarian, Italo-Albanian, Macedonian, Russian. (cc. 174-176)

Eastern Ecclesiastical Territorial Divisions in the Diaspora

In the (so-called) diaspora there are Eastern jurisdictions, such as apostolic exarchies and eparchies that correspond to apostolic vicariates and Latin dioceses and, in some cases, Eastern ordinariates. Eparchies are sometimes joined in one metropolitan structure. Otherwise, an Eastern eparchy may depend on a Latin metropolitan see. Eastern bishops constituted outside the territorial boundaries of their patriarchal or major archiepiscopal Church are members of the local and national conferences of bishops. Those bishops belonging to a patriarchal or major archiepiscopal Church are also members of their respective synods of bishop (CCEO c. 102), and those belonging to a metropolitan Church *sui iuris*, wherever they are constituted, are members of the council of hierarchs (CCEO c. 164).

The naming of bishops for individual territorial divisions is made by papal appointment upon the presentation of candidates by the synods of the patriarchal or major archiepiscopal Churches or by the council of hierarchs of the metropolitan Churches *sui iuris* (CCEO cc. 149, 168). The patriarchs and the major archbishops are competent to ordain and to enthrone metropolitans and bishops constituted outside of the territorial boundaries of their Church, unless it is expressly established otherwise (CCEO c. 86, §2). The same right to ordain and to enthrone bishops belongs to the metropolitan of the Church *sui iuris* in which he presides (CCEO c. 159).

The Congregation for the Eastern Churches, after an accurate evaluation of the circumstances and in consultation (*collatis consiliis*) with either the Congregation for Bishops or the Congregation for the Evangelization of Peoples (depending on which dicastery has jurisdiction over the territory), can propose to the Roman Pontiff the erection of a new Eastern eparchy or exarchy (CCEO c. 177 §2; PB 59). In dealing with these matters, the current praxis of the Holy See is to consult the competent Eastern hierarchies as well as the local Latin conferences of bishops.

See *Latin Metropolitans and Eastern Bishops in the Diaspora.*

Eastern Rites

Notion

A rite is not only a set of practices, prescriptions and customs, but "a liturgical, theological, spiritual and disciplinary heritage, differentiated by the culture and the circumstances of the history of peoples, which is expressed by each Church *sui iuris* in its own manner of living the faith" (CCEO c. 28 §1). Although noteworthy from various perspectives, a rite is not a constitutive juridical element of a Church *sui iuris*. In this sense, a rite is something that belongs to a person and follows that person wherever he or she dwells. A rite is not a juridic person with duties and rights, whereas a Church *sui iuris* is, with a very determinate physical person as its head and father. Thus, a rite is not synonymous with a Church.

As a heritage, however, a rite marks the identity of each Eastern Church *sui iuris* and of the Latin Church as well. The very concept of *ecclesia sui iuris*, even before the acknowledgment of its juridical status by the supreme authority of the Church, is marked out by its history, its culture and its *ritus*, that is, its sacred heritage developed during the centuries.

Division

In the Catholic Church, the rites arose in the West from the Roman tradition and in the East from the Alexandrian, Antiochian, Armenian, Chaldean and Constantinopolitan traditions (CCEO c. 28, §2). The Eastern traditions, prototypes of several rites, are three within the Roman Empire: Alexandria, Antioch (with Jerusalem), and Constantinople (with Cappadocia); and two at the margins of the Empire: the Syro-Oriental for Mesopotamia and Persia, and the Armenian emerging from the Antiochian and Constantinopolitan traditions.

Juridically, there are various Churches *sui iuris* deriving from the same *ritus* (as patrimony), but *de facto* there are many Churches with their own rite within the same tradition. Each of the Eastern Churches *sui iuris* may be traced to one of the five major traditions. Yet, with the exception of the Armenian Church, which coincides with its Armenian tradition, all the other Eastern Churches *sui iuris* of the same tradition have their own specific rite. For instance, the Russian, Bulgarian and Romanian Churches, even though they follow the Byzantine Rite, are diversified from each other, not only because each of them has a proper hierarchy and organic structure, but also because of all that is unique to the three cultures in which the Byzantine Rite has been harmoniously amalgamated (inculturation).

Rite of Baptism and Ascription to a Church Sui Iuris
   As a rule, with the reception of baptism Christian faithful are juridically ascribed to a Church *sui iuris* where they live and celebrate the faith according to the same Church patrimony, as described by c. 28, §1. Indeed, baptism must be celebrated according to the liturgical prescripts of the Church *sui iuris* in which the person to be baptized is to be ascribed in accord with the norm of law (CCEO c. 683).

See *Eastern Churches Sui Iuris; Ascription of Adults to be baptized to a Church Sui Iuris.*

Faculties/Competence of the Congregation for the Eastern Churches

Matters Reserved to the Roman Pontiff:
   The Congregation, within its proper and territorial competence, deals with the procedure in hand and prepares the proposal for decision by the Holy Father in the following cases:

- Concession of the *"communio ecclesiastica"* to the patriarchs canonically elected by their synods (CCEO c. 76, §2);
- When the election of a patriarch is not brought to completion within fifteen days from the opening of the synod of bishops of the patriarchal Church and the matter therefore devolves to the Roman Pontiff (CCEO c. 72, §2);
- Confirmation of the major archbishops canonically elected by their synods (CCEO c. 153, §§2-3);
- Previous assent to candidates to the episcopate legitimately proposed by the synods of the patriarchal and major archiepiscopal Churches or the assent to bishops legitimately elected (CCEO cc. 182, §3; 185, §1);
- Nomination and transfer of bishops and apostolic exarchs of the patriarchal and major archiepiscopal Churches *extra territorium proprium* and those of other Churches *sui iuris* (CCEO cc. 155, §1; 168; 181, §2; 149; 174-176; 314, §1);
- Nomination of ordinaries for the Eastern faithful without their own hierarchy, with due regard for CCEO c. 916, §5;

- Erection of patriarchal, major archiepiscopal, metropolitan *sui iuris* and all other Churches *sui iuris* (CCEO cc. 57, §1; 151; 155, §2; 174-176);
- Erection, modification, and suppression of eparchies and exarchies *extra territoria patriarchalia* (CCEO c. 177, §2);
- Nomination of apostolic administrators, apostolic visitors, and apostolic delegates;
- Prior consultation with the Roman Pontiff for the acceptance of the resignation of the patriarch by the synod of bishops of a patriarchal Church (CCEO c. 126, §2);
- Prior assent of the Roman Pontiff for the transfer of the patriarchl see (CCEO c. 57, §3);
- Prior assent of the Roman Pontiff for the nomination of a patriarchal procurator to the Holy See (CCEO c. 61);
- Acts regarding laws and decisions by the synod of bishops of the patriarchal Church that are sent to the Roman Pontiff as soon as possible (CCEO c. 111, §3);
- Dispensations from the impediments of sacred orders reserved to the Roman Pontiff (CCEO c. 795, §2);
- Exemption of institutes of consecrated life from the governance of the eparchial bishop to papal right (CCEO c. 412, §2);

Matters Entrusted to the Congregation:
Hierarchy and Clergy

- Prior consultation of the patriarch and major archbishop to erect provinces and eparchies, modify their boundaries, unite, divide, and suppress them, modify their hierarchical status, and transfer eparchial sees (CCEO c. 85, §1);
- Approval for the designation of a metropolitan for the eparchial bishop who exercises his power outside of the territorial boundaries of the patriarchal Church (CCEO c. 139);
- Assent for the designation of the proper hierarch for the Christian faithful of a Church *sui iuris* in places where there is none (CCEO c. 916, §5);
- Nomination of a visitor or delegate of the Congregation for the Eastern Churches;
- Assent for the nomination of a patriarchal visitor for the Christian faithful who reside outside of the territorial boundaries of a patriarchal Church (CCEO c. 148, §1);
- Approval for the laws or decisions of the synod of bishops of the patriarchal and major archiepiscopal Church to have the force of law everywhere in the world (CCEO c. 150, §3);
- Transmittal of the statutes drawn up by the council of hierarchs of the metropolitan Church *sui iuris* (CCEO c. 171);

- Recourse against an administrative decree of a patriarch or major archbishop when the question is referred to the Holy See (CCEO c. 1006);
- Recourse against the decisions of all local hierarchs established *extra territoria patriarchalia;*
- Recourse against the administrative decrees of an exarch who governs an exarchy in the name of the Roman Pontiff (CCEO c. 316);
- Approval of the statutes of the assemblies of hierarchs of several Churches *sui iuris* (CCEO c. 322, §4);
- Preparation of the *ad limina* visits of the Eastern and Latin bishops of the territories of competence of the Congregation (PB 31-32);
- Erection, approval or suppression of public associations of Christian faithful which are neither eparchial nor patriarchal (CCEO cc. 575, §1, 3°; 583, §1);
- Suppression of juridic persons erected or approved by the Holy See (CCEO c. 928, 3°);
- Determination or formation of missionary territories and direction of apostolic and missionary activity in regions where Eastern rites have been preponderant from ancient times, even if carried out by Latin missionaries (PB 60; CCEO c. 594);
- Determination of the maximum amount for the alienation of ecclesiastical goods and consent for the alienation when the value of the goods exceeds said amount as well as when dealing with precious goods or goods given to the Church by vow, without prejudice to the competence of the synod of bishops within the patriarchal or major archiepiscopal territory (CCEO c. 1036);
- Consent for the alienation of ecclesiastical goods and the terms and conditions of contract that could cause damage to the patrimonial situation of the ecclesiastical juridic person, in Egypt, Jordan, Greece, Iran, Iraq, Israel, the Palestinian Territories, Lebanon, Syria and Turkey.

Liturgy and Sacraments

- Previous review (*recognitio*) of the liturgical texts, after the *nihil obstat* from the Congregation for the Doctrine of Faith (CCEO c. 657);
- Faculty of bi-ritualism to celebrate the Divine Liturgy/Mass and the sacraments according to the liturgical prescripts of another Church *sui iuris* (CCEO c. 674, §2);
- Adaptation to another rite different from one's own;
- Permission for a local bishop to ordain a candidate subject to him who is ascribed to another Church *sui iuris* (CCEO c. 748, §2; CIC c. 1015);
- Permission for the celebration of baptism according to the liturgical prescripts of the Church *sui iuris* in which, in accord with the norm of law, the person to be baptized is to be ascribed (CCEO c. 683);
- Dispensation beyond a year from the age required by common law to receive sacred orders, with due regard for competence of patriarchs and

major archbishops within the territorial boundaries of their Churches (CCEO c. 759, §2);

- Dispensation beyond a year from philosophical-theological studies for those who are destined for the priesthood, with the obligation to complete said studies (CCEO c. 348, §1);
- Dispensation from the impediments to receive or exercise sacred orders for those persons who have attempted marriage, even only civilly; those who have committed voluntary homicide or who have procured a completed abortion, and all persons who positively cooperated in either; those who have seriously and maliciously mutilated themselves or another person, or who have attempted suicide; those who have performed an act of sacred orders that has been reserved to clerics; and those who hold an office or position of administration that is forbidden to clerics (CCEO c. 762, §1, 2°-7°); all the above with the due competence of the patriarchs and major archbishops within the territorial boundaries of their respective Churches (CCEO c. 767, §2);
- Prior consultation to establish new diriment impediments in the particular law of a Church *sui iuris* (CCEO c. 792);
- Addition of an invalidating clause by the local hierarch, prohibiting a member of the Christian faithful, in a particular case, from entering marriage *extra territoria patriachalia* (CCEO c. 794);
- Dispensation from canonical form for the celebration of marriage, with due regard to the competence of the patriarchs and major archbishops within the territories of their Churches (CCEO c. 835);
- Concession of a radical sanation, without the obligation to renew matrimonial consent, of a marriage invalid because of an impediment reserved to the Holy See or an impediment of divine law that has now ceased, or of a mixed marriage when the conditions prescribed by law have not been fulfilled (CCEO cc. 852; 814);
- Approval of the particular law of a Church *sui iuris* by which certain festive days of obligation are suppressed or transferred to a Sunday (CCEO c. 880, §3);
- Reduction of the obligation of celebrating the Divine Liturgy (CCEO c. 1052, §1);
- Consent for the alienation or transfer of well-known relics, icons or images that are held in great veneration by the people in a particular Church (CCEO c. 888, §2).
- On January 6, 1996, the Congregaton for the Eastern Churches published an Instruction for the application of the liturgical prescriptions of the Code of Canons of the Eastern Churches (Liturgical Instruction). This Liturgical Instruction brings together in an organic framework the liturgical norms to be observed by all the Eastern Catholic Churches. At the same time, it sets forth the principles for the development of liturgical directories of the individual Churches *sui iuris* and exhorts them to organize in an appropriate way the liturgical formation of clergy and laity.

Religious life

- Erection of an Eastern house or province of a Latin religious institute (CCEO c. 432);
- Approval of the *typica* or statutes of monasteries, orders and congregations of pontifical right, dispensation from the same *typica* or statutes, and implementation of canonical visitation (CCEO c. 414, §2);
- Erection or suppression of monasteries of pontifical right (CCEO c. 434; c. 438, §4); approval of confederations among monasteries *sui iuris* that are neither eparchial nor patriarchal (CCEO c. 439, §3). The Congregation decides on the disposition of the goods of a suppressed monastery of pontifical right (CCEO c. 438, §4);
- Prior consultation for the erection of a congregation of eparchial right (CCEO c. 506, §1);
- Prior consultation for the erection of orders and congregations by a patriarch or a major archbishop (CCEO c. 506, §2);
- Prior consultation for the erection of a monastery of eparchial right *extra territoria patriarchalia* (CCEO c. 435, §1);
- Approval of new forms of consecrated life (CCEO c. 571);
- Consent for the suppression of a congregation of patriarchal, major archiepiscopal, or eparchial right (CCEO c. 507, §2);
- Suppression of an order, even if of patriarchal right; the Congregation decides on the disposition of the goods of the suppressed order (CCEO c. 507, §1);
- Suppression of monasteries *sui iuris* or filial monasteries outside of the boundaries of patriarchal or major archiepiscopal territories (CCEO c. 438, §2);
- Admission of candidates to a religious institute of another Church *sui iuris* (CCEO cc. 451; 517, §2; 559);
- Consent for the validity of the transfer to a monastery of another Church *sui iuris* (CCEO cc. 487, §4; 544, §4; 562, §1)
- Indult to leave a monastery, an order or a congregation, for members in perpetual vows (CCEO cc. 492, §1; 549, §2);
- Approval of the decree of dismissal of a member in perpetual vows (CCEO cc. 500, §4; 553);
- Permission for the canonical regularization of Eastern faithful admitted into institutes of another Church *sui iuris* (CCEO cc. 451; 517, §2);
- Addressing a legitimate recourse against a decree of dismissal, submitted by the interested party within 15 days *extra territoria patriarchalia* (CCEO c. 501 §3);
- Recourse against the decisions of a religious superior within the canonical terms.

Other Matters

- Recourse for the reduction, moderation, or commutation of the wills of the Christian faithful who give their goods for pious causes (CCEO c. 1054, §3);

- Legitimation of illegitimate children (CIC c. 1139);
- Consent to transfer to another Church *sui iuris* (CCEO cc. 32, §1; 34; 36-37);
- Admission of an Eastern non-Catholic into the Latin Church (CCEO cc. 35-36; 897);
- Appointment of the Staff of the Pontifical Eastern Colleges.

Matters for the Congregation's Information:

- When the patriarch or major archbishop, within their territorial boundaries and with the consent of the synod of bishops, appoints an eparchial or coadjutor or auxiliary bishop in accord with the canonical norms (CCEO cc. 181, §1; 182-187; 212); when the same transfers a metropolitan, eparchial or titular bishop to another see (if any of these refuse, the matter is deferred to the Roman Pontiff); and when the same, with the consent of the permanent synod, erects, modifies and suppresses exarchies (CCEO c. 85, §2-4);
- When a bishop is elected in a patriarchal or major archiepiscopal Church, and the one elected is on the list of candidates to which the Roman Pontiff has already given assent (CCEO c. 184);
- When an eparchial see becomes vacant (CCEO c. 220, 1°);
- When, for a serious reason, a permanent synod cannot be constituted (CCEO c. 121);
- When laws and norms are enacted by the council of hierarchs of a metropolitan Church *sui iuris* (CCEO c. 167, §2);
- When the quinquennial report on the state of the eparchy or exarchy is submitted to the patriarch or major archbishop, it is also to be sent to the Holy See (CCEO cc. 206; 318, §2); the same is done by the superiors of patriarchal and eparchial religious institutes (CCEO cc. 318, §2; 419, §2);
- When eparchial/diocesan bishops provide for the spiritual needs of the Christian faithful of another Church *sui iuris* by means of presbyters or pastors or syncelli of the same Church *sui iuris* (CCEO c. 193, §3; CIC c. 383, §2).

Furthermore, the Congregation presents to the Roman Pontiff any other matters *maioris momenti.*

In addition, the Congregation supervises the proper training of Eastern students everywhere and of Latin ones in the territories of its jurisdiction. The formation of candidates for holy orders is also promoted by means of appropriate directives, scholarships and the maintenance of educational institutions according to the specific tradition of their ritual affiliation. The Congregation is constantly providing much needed moral and financial support to all the Eastern Churches.

Formation of Eastern Faithful according to Their Own Rite

The Vatican II Constitution on the Sacred Liturgy, *Sacrosanctum concilium*, declares: "The Church very much wants all faithful to be led to take a full, conscious and active part in liturgical celebration. This is demanded by the nature of the liturgy itself; and, by virtue of their baptism, it is the right and the duty of the Christian people, the chosen race, the royal priesthood, the holy nation, and the people of whom God has taken possession" (SC 14). Therefore, "the Church devotes careful efforts to prevent Christian faithful from attending this mystery of faith as though they were outsiders or silent onlookers: rather, having a good understanding of this mystery, through the ritual and the prayers, they should share in the worshipping event, aware of what is happening and devoutly involved. They should be formed by God's word" (SC 48).

Furthermore, the Decree on the Eastern Catholic Churches, *Orientalium ecclesiarum*, asserts: "All Eastern Christians should know and be certain that they may and should always preserve their own lawful liturgical rites and way of life, and that changes should be made only by reason of their proper and organic development. All these things are to be observed with the greatest fidelity by the Eastern Christians themselves. They should indeed, from day to day, acquire greater knowledge of these matters and more perfect practice of them and if for reasons of circumstances, times or persons they have fallen unduly short of this they should have recourse to their age-old traditions" (OE 6).

Later on, the same conciliar decree explicitly recommends that those persons who, by reason of their office or an apostolic ministry, have frequent contact with the Eastern Churches or their faithful are to be carefully instructed in the knowledge and practice of the rites, law, teaching, history and nature of Eastern Christians, in keeping with the importance of the office they hold.

The Eastern code converts this recommendation into a canonical norm that binds the Latin Church as well: "The Christian faithful of any Church *sui iuris*, even of the Latin Church, who by reason of their office, ministry, or function have frequent dealings with the Christian faithful of another Church *sui iuris*, are to have an accurate formation in the knowledge and practice of the rite of the same Church in keeping with the importance of the office, ministry or function they hold" (CCEO c. 41).

Canon 17 endorses the right of the Eastern Christian faithful to worship God according to the prescriptions of their own Church *sui iuris* and to follow their own form of spirituality in accord with the teaching of the Church. Equally, the Latin code asserts that the Christian faithful have the right to worship God according to the prescripts of their own rite approved by the legitimate pastors of the Church and to follow their own form of spirituality so long as it is consonant with the doctrine of the Church (CIC c. 214).

With this perspective in mind, the Eastern code, in order to avoid possible difficulties in the exercise of this right, makes it clear: "No one is to presume to induce in any way the Christian faithful to transfer to another Church *sui iuris*" (CCEO c. 31). In fact, c. 1465 establishes a penalty as follows: "A person who, ascribed to any Church *sui iuris*, including the Latin Church, and exercising an office, a ministry or another function in the Church, has presumed to induce any member of the Christian faithful whatsoever to transfer to another Church *sui iuris* contrary to c. 31, is to be punished with an appropriate penalty."

Missionary Action of the Eastern Catholic Churches

Vatican II Principles

In the Decree *Orientalium ecclesiarum*, the council fathers, referring to the Churches of both the East and the West, solemnly declared that, "although they differ somewhat in what are called rites, such as liturgy, ecclesiastical discipline and spiritual heritage, still they are entrusted on equal footing to the pastoral guidance of the Roman Pontiff, who by divine right succeeds blessed Peter in the primacy over the whole Church. Thus the same Churches enjoy equal dignity, so that none of them ranks higher than the others by reason of rite, and they enjoy the same rights and are bound by the same laws, even as regards preaching the Gospel throughout the whole world (Mark 16:15), under the direction of the Roman Pontiff " (OE 3).

Canonical Norm

This conciliar declaration becomes for the Eastern Catholic Churches a demanding missionary imperative as it is confirmed by the new Eastern code. In fact, c. 585 states that, "it is for each Church *sui iuris* continually to take care that, through suitably prepared preachers sent by a competent authority in accord with the norms of the common law, the Gospel is preached in the whole world under the guidance of the Roman Pontiff."

The synod of bishops of the patriarchal and major archiepiscopal Churches, as well as the council of hierarchs of the metropolitan Churches *sui iuris*, have the right to establish norms for missionary activity. Moreover, the legislator exhorts the Eastern faithful to foster in them and others love toward the missions, to pray for them, to encourage vocations, and to generously support the missions with their donations.

Since the task to announce the Gospel *ad omnes gentes* falls primarily on the episcopal body, the direction and coordination of missionary work belongs to the supreme authority of the Church that is to the Roman Pontiff and the college of bishops. The Roman Pontiff avails himself of the services of the Congregation for the Evangelization of Peoples. In fact, the history of the missionary activity of the Catholic Church formally began with the institution of the Congregation *de Propaganda Fide*.

The conciliar decree on the missionary activity of the Church, *Ad gentes*, dealing with the general organization of missionary work, states: "For all missions and for all missionary activity there should be only one competent congregation, namely that of "Propagation of the Faith," by which both missionary activity itself and missionary cooperation should be directed and coordinated all over the world. The rights, however, of the Eastern Churches must be respected" (AG 29).

Footnote 10 of chapter 5 adds: "If any missions, for some special reason, are still temporarily under the control of other curial departments, it is desirable that these departments should be in contact with the Congregation for Propagation of the Faith, so that in the organization and direction of all missions there may be standards and norms that are completely constant and uniform." It is then hoped that, "this congregation should be both an instrument of administration and an organ of dynamic direction, which makes use of scientific methods and instruments which are appropriate to the circumstances of our time, taking account, that is, of modern theological inquiry and of the methodology and pastoral nature of missionary work" (AG 29).

Competence of the Congregation for the Eastern Churches

All the above is confirmed by the apostolic constitution on the Roman curia, *Pastor Bonus,* in article 85: "It pertains to the Congregation for the Evangelization of Peoples to direct and coordinate throughout the world the actual work of spreading the Gospel as well as missionary cooperation, without prejudice to the competence of the Congregation for the Eastern Churches." As for the competence of the Congregation for the Eastern Churches in regard to missionary activity, the same apostolic constitution states: "In regions where Eastern rites have been preponderant from ancient times, apostolic and missionary activity depends solely on this Congregation, even if it is carried out by missionaries of the Latin Church" (PB 60).

Missionary Activity by Eastern Missionaries in Latin Mission Territories

Today, instances of Latin ordinaries' in mission territories entrusting pastoral tasks to missionaries of Eastern Catholic Churches, particularly religious members of Eastern institutes, are not rare. If a religious institute intends to erect a Latin house in its mission territory, it must, in accord with c. 432 of the Eastern code, obtain the previous consent of the Holy See. In other cases, the permission of the local ordinary is sufficient, with the proviso that community life and the internal governance of the house is regulated by the constitutions and particular law of the proper Church *sui iuris* (CCEO c. 437; CIC c. 611). Eastern missionary clerics are also required to obtain from the Congregation for the Eastern Churches accommodation to the Latin rite or at least an indult of bi-ritualism, in order to celebrate the religious functions licitly according to the Latin rite.

See *Adaptation of Rite; Biritualism; Eastern Houses and Provinces of Latin Religious Institutes; Catechumens.*

OTHER

Adoption of Minors

Principle

Children who have been adopted according to the norm of civil law are considered canonically the children of those who have adopted them (CIC c. 110), that is, the adoptive parents enjoy full parental legal rights.

Legal State of the Adopted Children

As to the legal state of an adopted minor who has not yet completed fourteen years of age, one must refer to CCEO c. 29, §2, 2°, in relation with c. 29 §1. The adopted son or daughter who has not yet completed fourteen years of age by virtue of baptism is ascribed to the Church *sui iuris* to which the Catholic adoptive father is ascribed; if only the mother is Catholic, or if both parents are of the same mind in requesting it, to the Church *sui iuris* to which the adoptive mother is ascribed, without prejudice to particular law enacted by the Holy See (CCEO c. 29, §2, 2°).

The following are some cases that have arisen as a result of the wars in the Balkans and of the fall of the communist regimes in Central and Eastern Europe, since Catholic families in the West have adopted a great number of children from those regions.

- A non-baptized minor who has not yet completed fourteen years of age, by virtue of adoption becomes the son or daughter of the adoptive parents; therefore, with the reception of baptism he or she belongs to the Church of the adopting Catholic parents, Latin or Eastern, in accordance with the CCEO c. 29, §1; CIC c. 111, §1). If the adopting parents belong to different Churches *sui iuris*, the adopted son or daughter is ascribed to the Church of the father; if both parents are of the same mind, he or she is ascribed to the Church of the mother.
- A child baptized in the Church of his or her natural Catholic parents, Latin or Eastern, is already ascribed to that Church, in compliance with c. 29, §1 of the Eastern code and c. 111, §1 of the Latin code. Children who have been adopted according to the norm of civil law are considered the children of the person or persons who have adopted them. A child who has not yet completed the fourteen years of age, automatically belongs to the Church *sui iuris* of the adopting Catholic parents, Latin or Eastern, in accordance with the same just mentioned canons. If the adopting parents belong to different Churches, the adopted child is ascribed to the father's Church; if both parents are of the same mind, the child is ascribed to the Church of the mother. Thus, a minor who has been baptized in an Eastern Catholic Church *sui iuris* and is later on adopted by Latin spouses is ascribed to the Latin Church. It is not necessary to obtain the consent of the Holy See for the transfer to the Latin Church, as requested by the CCEO c. 32 and CIC c. 112, §1, 1°. The same is true for the reverse case. Nevertheless, upon completion of

the child's fourteenth year of age, he or she can choose to return to the original Church of the natural parents, following by analogy the norms in CCEO c. 34 and CIC c. 112, §1, 3°.

- A child of Orthodox or Protestant parents, who has been baptized in his or her respective Church or Ecclesial Community and is later on adopted by Catholic parents, Latin or Eastern, is ascribed to the Church of the adopting Catholic parents, provided that he or she has not yet completed the fourteenth year of age. In this case, c. 35 of the Eastern code does not apply to the non-Catholics who enter into full communion with the Catholic Church and are ascribed to the Church *sui iuris* of the same rite; the applicable canon in the Eastern code is c. 29, §2, 2°, which refers to paragraph 1 of the same c. 29 (see also CIC c. 111, §1). In practice, said minor is ascribed to the Latin Church if he or she is legitimately adopted by Latin Catholic parents, or to the Eastern Catholic Church *sui iuris* of his or her adopting parents.
- A child who is born of Orthodox parents and adopted by Catholic spouses, Latin or Eastern, and whose Orthodox baptism is uncertain is to be baptized conditionally (CCEO c. 672, §2; CIC c. 845, §2). In this case, if the child has not yet completed the fourteenth year of age, he or she is ascribed to the adopting parents' Church, in compliance with c. 29, §§1-2, 2° of the Eastern code and cc. 110-111, §1 of the Latin code.

See *Ascription to a Church Sui Iuris of Children Under 14 Years of Age; Baptism (Orthodox and Protestant).*

Alienation of Goods Reserved to the Holy See

Canon law is not, in principle, favorable to the alienation of ecclesiastical goods, especially when they are a permanent patrimony of the Church. For a just cause, however, and under certain circumstances, such transactions may be allowed (CCEO c. 1035; CIC cc. 1291, 1293). In fact, it could be justified as beneficial or even necessary in the light of the mission of the juridic person in question. Good administration, though, must take into account all the regulations of the civil society on the matter.

The alienation of ecclesiastical goods, in the proper sense, is the transfer of ownership; it differs radically from the administration of goods. The ownership that is alienated may be total (as in fee simple ownership of real estate) or partial (as in a life estate or a remainder interest in real estate). It is effected nearly always by sale, gift, or exchange.

One can also speak of alienation in an improper sense when no transfer of ownership takes place. Mortgaging property is not, strictly speaking, an act of alienation. The same is true of assuming a mortgage when purchasing property which already has a mortgage on it. Granting a right of way or an easement to cross or otherwise use one's land, since it does not involve a transfer of ownership, is not an act of strict alienation. Nor is leasing, or granting an option to purchase one's property, or borrowing or loaning sums of money with or without collateral, or refusing a gift.

The validity of alienation requires the permission of the competent ecclesiastical authority, which varies according to the value of the goods in question (CCEO cc. 1036-1037; CIC c. 1292). In each case the value must be specified by experts in writing (CCEO cc. 1035, §1, 2°; CIC c. 1293, §1, 2°).

The synod of bishops of the patriarchal and major archiepiscopal Churches must establish for their own ecclesiastical territories, the minimum and maximum sums relative to the value of the goods to be alienated. Outside of the patriarchal and archiepiscopal territory, the amount of the minimum and maximum is set by the Holy See or the local episcopal conference.

The Eastern code c. 1036, §1-3, in dealing with the alienation of goods of juridic persons of the patriarchal and major archiepiscopal Church within its own territory, does not foresee any intervention of the Holy See. When the value of the goods is above the maximum sum or even double, it is up to the patriarch with his synod, respectively the permanent synod or the synod of bishops, to consent or not to such alienation.

Outside of the territory of a patriarchal or major archiepiscopal Church, c. 1036, §4 requires the consent of the Holy See for the alienation *ad validitatem* "if the value of the goods exceeds the amount established or approved by the Holy See itself and if it concerns precious goods or goods given to the Church by vow." The Latin code c. 1292, §2 expresses practically the same norm as the CCEO, with the difference that the maximum sum for the alienation is established by the local episcopal conference. The competent authorities of the juridic persons of the Eastern Catholic Churches must obtain the permission from the Congregation for the Eastern Churches. This Congregation has the faculty to grant such permission even to the juridic persons of the Latin Church within the territories under its jurisdiction.

The alienation of ecclesiastical goods in the Middle East is regulated by the special norms established by Pope Paul VI in the early 1970's and renewed by Pope John Paul II on July 6, 1995, subsequent to the promulgation of the Eastern code. According to papal dispositions, the alienation of any property of juridic persons, Latin or Eastern, is prohibited without the explicit authorization of the Holy See, let alone any contract *quo condicio patrimonialis personae iuridicae peior fieri potest.* As for the latter case, such a risk includes mortgages, loans, long term leases (ten years and up), and renewable short term leases, or transactions where one adopts for a freehold property the system of the key money in the form of a security deposit. This prohibition applies to Egypt, Jordan, Greece, Iran, Iraq, Israel, Palestinian Territories, Lebanon, Syria and Turkey; and, as in the prior case, the Congregation for the Eastern Churches is competent to grant the authorization.

As for the purchase of goods, no particular authorization from the Holy See is needed, provided that the purchaser, in order to satisfy the vendor, does not have to go into debt or mortgage or sell patrimonial goods, or assume an onerous burden for the juridic person. In this case, to avoid putting the juridic person's patrimony at risk, the same formalities required for alienation must be observed (CCEO c. 1042; CIC c. 1295), including, for the nations of the Middle East, the special authorization of the Holy See.

The *Nota explicativa* of February 12, 2004, by the Pontifical Council for the Interpretation of Legislative Texts, establishes that "when the Holy See gives permission for an alienation of ecclesiastical goods, it does not assume the eventual economic responsibilities inherent to that alienation, but only guarantees that the alienation in question is congruent with the end of the ecclesiastical patrimony." In this way is proper vigilance exercised for the correct administration and use of the Church's goods.

Causes for Canonization

Canon 1057 of the Eastern code prescribes that in causes of canonization of the servants of God the special norms established by the Holy See are to be observed. A similar norm is found in the Latin code c. 1403. According to the apostolic constitution *Pastor Bonus* (PB 71-74), the Congregation for the Causes of the Saints deals with everything that leads to the canonization of the servants of God, whether they belong to Eastern Churches *sui iuris* or to the Latin Church. Moreover, it has competence to decide everything concerning the authentication of holy relics and their preservation.

Catholic Universities and Faculties

For the distinction in current legislation between Catholic universities and ecclesiastical faculties, one must turn to the Second Vatican Council's Declaration on Christian Education, *Gravissimum educationis* (1965) and to the Apostolic Constitution on Ecclesiastical Universities and Faculties, *Sapientia Christiana* (1979), which clearly differentiate these two institutions on the basis of their specific nature and purpose.

Catholic Universities

Even if it is in fact Catholic, no university of studies is to bear the title or name of *Catholic university* without the consent of the competent ecclesiastical authority (CIC c. 808). In the Latin Church the competent ecclesiastical authority is the Congregation for Catholic Education or the conference of bishops with prior due consultation: a Catholic university is an institute of higher studies that has been publicly erected or approved by the Holy See or the conference of bishops.

In the Eastern Churches, a Catholic university is an institute of higher studies that is erected as such or is approved either by the higher administrative authority of a Church *sui iuris* after previous consultation with the Holy See or by the Holy See itself. The university's erection or approval must be established by a public document. Within the territorial boundaries of a patriarchal Church the higher authority is the patriarch with the consent of the synod of bishops (CCEO c. 642).

Ecclesiastical Universities and Faculties

Ecclesiastical universities or faculties, which are to study the sacred disciplines and those connected with the sacred and to instruct students scientifically in the same disciplines, are proper to the Church by virtue of its function to announce the revealed truth (CIC c. 815). Hierarchs, above all, should constantly strive to promote ecclesiastical universities and faculties, that is, those that deal especially with Christian revelation and the sciences connected with it and so are closely linked with the Church's function of evangelization (CCEO c. 646).

The Holy See, through the Congregation for Catholic Education, works to ensure that there is in the Church a sufficient number of ecclesiastical and Catholic universities, as well as other educational institutions, in which the sacred disciplines may be pursued in depth and studies in the humanities and the sciences may be promoted, with due regard for Christian truth, so that the Christian faithful may be suitably trained to fulfill their own tasks (PB art. 116, §1).

In the Latin Church, ecclesiastical universities and faculties can be established only through erection by the Holy See or with its approval, and are subject to its supervision. Individual ecclesiastical universities and faculties must have their own statutes and plan of studies approved by the Holy See (CIC c. 816).

Mandate to Teach Theological Disciplines

Those who teach theological disciplines in any institutes of higher studies whatsoever must have a mandate from the competent ecclesiastical authority. The same authority can withdraw this mandate for a serious cause, especially if the teachers lack scientific or pedagogical suitability, experience, or integrity of doctrine (CIC c. 812; CCEO c. 644).

The "mandate to teach" is not only a public endorsement of the sound doctrine taught by the teacher in full communion with the Church, but also that the teacher is officially empowered to do so by the ecclesiastical authority and therefore joined in a greater degree to the teaching authority. For this reason, if the mandate is withdrawn due to disagreement with the magisterium, the teacher can no longer teach in ecclesiastical universities and faculties and is considered unsuitable to teach Catholic theology. "Those who teach matters touching on faith and the morals are to be conscious of their duty to carry out their work in full communion with the authentic magisterium of the Church, above all, with that of the Roman Pontiff" (Ap. Const. *Sapientia Christiana* art. 26, §2).

Ecclesial Assemblies

In governing the Churches *sui iuris* and the individual eparchies, hierarchs can use, as a means of consultation and to favor greater ecclesial communion, special assemblies that represent all its members.

Patriarchal Assembly

The patriarchal assembly is a consultative group of the entire Church presided over by the patriarch. It assists the patriarch and the synod of bishops of the patriarchal Church in dealing with matters of major importance, in particular, to harmonize the forms and methods of the apostolate as well as ecclesiastical discipline, adapting them to the current circumstances of the time and to the common good of the respective Church, but also taking into account the entire territory where several Churches *sui iuris* coexist (CCEO c. 140).

The patriarchal assembly is to be convoked at least every five years and whenever the patriarch, with the consent of the permanent synod or the synod of bishops of the patriarchal Church, considers it to be useful (CCEO c. 141).

Members of another Church *sui iuris,* including the Latin Church, can be invited to the patriarchal assembly and participate in it, in accordance with the statutes. Observers from other Churches or non-Catholic Ecclesial Communities can also be invited to the patriarchal assembly (CCEO c. 143, §§3-4).

Assemblies of Other Churches Sui Iuris

What the law states about the assembly of the patriarchal Church is deemed applicable to the assemblies of major archiepiscopal Churches (CCEO c. 152) and metropolitan Churches *sui iuris* (CCEO c. 172). In point of fact, the other Eastern Catholic Churches *sui iuris* also periodically convene their assembly, called either a provincial synod or an inter-eparchial synod. Since such an organ is not foreseen by law, its convocation is to be authorized by the Holy See, which also approves its decisions.

Eparchial Assembly

The eparchial assembly assists the eparchial bishop in matters pertaining to the special needs of the eparchy and its benefits (CCEO c. 235). The eparchial assembly is convoked when, in the judgment of the eparchial bishop and after consultation with the presbyteral council, circumstances recommend it (CCEO c. 236).

The eparchial bishop, if he judges it opportune, may invite others to the eparchial assembly, including persons of other Churches *sui iuris*, to all of whom he can even grant the right to vote. Observers from non-Catholic Churches or Ecclesial Communities may also be invited to the eparchial eparchy (CCEO c. 238, §§2-3).

The eparchial assembly corresponds to the diocesan synod in the Latin Church (CIC cc. 460-468). Canon 463, §3 authorizes the diocesan bishop, if he judges it opportune, to invite as observers to the diocesan synod other ministers or members of Churches or Ecclesial Communities not in full communion with the Catholic Church. This canon does not mention the members of the Eastern Catholic Churches *sui iuris*, but such an invitation is implied *ex ipsa natura rei.*

Ecclesiastical Communion

Theological Concept

"In full communion with the Catholic Church on this earth are those baptized persons who are joined with Christ in its visible structure by the bonds of the profession of faith, the sacraments and ecclesiastical governance" (CCEO c. 8; CIC c. 205). Consequently, "the Christian faithful are bound by an obligation in the manner of their conduct to maintain always communion with the Church" (CCEO c. 12; CIC c. 209). Both codes make ample reference to ecclesiastical communion:

- Hierarchical communion of the Roman Pontiff with all other bishops and indeed with the universal Church (CCEO c. 45, §2; CIC c. 333, §2).
- Hierarchical communion of the bishops with the head of the Roman See and the episcopal college (CCEO cc. 7, §2; 45, §2; 49; 597, §2; 600; CIC cc. 204, §2; 333, §2; 336; 749, §2; 753).
- Ecclesiastical communion of the patriarch with the Roman Pontiff (CCEO cc. 76, §2; 92, §1).

Ecclesiastical Communion of the Patriarch with the Roman Pontiff

The synod of bishops of the patriarchal Church is to inform the Roman Pontiff as soon as possible, by means of a synodal letter, that the election and enthronement were canonically carried out and that the profession of faith and promise to exercise his office faithfully were made by the new patriarch in the presence of the synod according to the approved formulas. Synodal letters about the election are also to be sent to the patriarchs of the other Eastern Churches. The new patriarch must request as soon as possible ecclesiastical communion from the Roman Pontiff by means of a letter signed in his own hand (CCEO c. 76).

The new patriarch, though canonically elected, validly exercises his office only after his enthronement, by which he obtains his office with the full effects of law. He is neither to convoke the synod of bishops of the patriarchal Church nor to ordain bishops before receiving *ecclesiastical communion* from the Roman Pontiff (CCEO c. 77).

Ecclesiastical communion is also manifested in liturgical services. Since the promulgation of the Eastern code, the earlier practice of imposing the pallium has been replaced by the Eucharistic concelebration of the newly elected patriarch with the Roman Pontiff or his delegate. As a sign of *full communion* with the Roman Pontiff, the patriarch commemorates him in the Divine Liturgy and the Divine Praises according to the prescriptions of the liturgical books; he is also to see that this is done faithfully by all the bishops and other clerics of his Church (CCEO c. 92, §2).

The patriarch manifests *hierarchical communion* with the successor of Saint Peter in the See of Rome, through the fidelity, reverence and obedience that are due to the supreme pastor of the entire Church. His dealings with the Roman Pontiff must be frequent, and he is to submit to him a report concerning the state of the Church over which he presides according to the special norms regarding the matter. Within a year of his election and afterwards several times during the tenure of his office, he is to visit the See of Rome to venerate the tombs of the Apostles Peter and Paul and to present himself to the successor of Peter in primacy over the entire Church (CCEO c. 92, §§1-3).

Ecclesiastical Dignities

The Roman Pontiff traditionally confers pontifical honors upon Catholic ecclesiastics as a sign of appreciation and recognition of the service they have rendered. The titles of Chaplain to His Holiness, Prelate of Honor to His Holiness and Protonotary Apostolic Supernumerary are conferred on diocesan/eparchial clergy worldwide. Requests must be submitted to the Apostolic Nuncio, who will forward said requests with his *nihil obstat* to the competent dicastery in Rome (Instruction on the Conferral of Pontifical Honors N° 16.846/ON – May 16, 2001).

Patriarchs and major archbishops can confer on any cleric an ecclesiastical honor recognized in their own Church *sui iuris*, provided they have the written consent of the eparchial/diocesan bishop to whom the cleric is subject (CCEO c. 89, §3). Patriarchs or major archbishops, within their own territory, can confer on any cleric, even of another rite, an ecclesiastical honor recognized in their own Church *sui iuris*, provided they have the written consent of the eparchial/diocesan bishop to whom the cleric is subject and the *nihil obstat* of the Congregation for the Eastern Churches (CCEO c. 89, §3).

Metropolitans of metropolitan Churches *sui iuris* can confer ecclesiastical honors only on clerics of the same Church, and eparchial bishops only on clerics subject them (CCEO c. 194). To confer dignities on clerics of another Church, both the written consent of the cleric's bishop and the *nihil obstat* of the Congregation for the Eastern Churches are required.

Clerics who receive honors according to these directives are permitted to use the rights and insignia associated with them within the territory of the grantor. Those who receive them from the Roman Pontiff may use them everywhere. In addition, taking into account the proviso of c. 388 of the Eastern code, dignities used in the Eastern Churches are not to be granted to clerics who do not belong to the Church *sui iuris* which confers them (LI 78).

Ecumenical Councils

An ecumenical council, an institution of ecclesiastical law, is linked to the college of bishops, which is of divine law. "This college, in so far as it is composed of many, expresses the variety and the universality of the people of God, but in so far it is gathered under one head it expresses the unity of the flock of Christ [...] The supreme power over the whole Church which this college enjoys is solemnly exercised in an ecumenical council" (LG 22). Ecumenical councils are extraordinary assemblies of the college of bishops of the entire Church. According to Catholic ecclesiology, only the Roman Pontiff is to convoke an ecumenical council, preside over it personally or through others, transfer, suspend, or dissolve it, and approve its decrees (CCEO c. 51; CIC c. 338).

All and only the bishops who are members of the college of bishops have the right and duty to take part in an ecumenical council with a deliberative vote. Others who are not bishops can be called to an ecumenical council by the supreme authority of the Church, to whom it belongs to determine their roles in the council. If the Holy See becomes vacant during the celebration of a council, the council is interrupted by virtue of the law itself until the new Roman Pontiff orders the ecumenical council to be continued or dissolves it. The decrees of an ecumenical council do not have obligatory force unless they are approved by the Roman Pontiff together with the council fathers, confirmed by him and promulgated at his order (CCEO cc. 52-54; CIC cc. 339-341).

The formula of approval, confirmation and promulgation of the Second Vatican Council documents is noteworthy: "Each and all of these matters which are laid down in the constitution/decree/declaration have been approved by the Fathers. And we, by the apostolic power given by Christ to us, and in union with the venerable Fathers, approve, decree and prescribe them in the Holy Spirit, and we order that what has been laid down by the council is to be promulgated to the glory of God: I, Paul, bishop of the Catholic Church" (*There follow the signatures of the Fathers*).

The traditional list of the first eight ecumenical councils informally recognized by the Catholic Church ends with the fourth ecumenical council held in Constantinople in 869 (Constantinople IV, 869-870). After the schism of 1054 and the consequent break of communion between the Christian East and Christian West, the general councils of the Middle Ages present a substantially different aspect not only in their limiting Latin boundary - with the exception of Lyons II and Florence - but also for other important aspects. The current Catholic listing since the Fourth Council of Constantinople is the following: Lateran I in 1123, Lateran II in 1139, Lateran III in 1179, Lateran IV in 1215, Lyons I in 1245, Lyons II in 1274, Vienne in 1311, Constance in 1414, Florence in 1438, Lateran V in 1512, Trent in 1545, Vatican I in 1869 and Vatican II in 1962.

Gypsies (Care of)

The ever-growing movement of gypsies and nomads to Eastern regions has gradually activated not only civil government agencies but also the Church, in its missionary outreach to them. This pastoral care of the Church for gypsies and nomads is prompted by its solicitude and zeal. The Eastern code exhorts eparchial bishops "to consider the non-baptized as being committed to him in the Lord and see that the love of Christ shines upon them from the witness of the Christian faithful living in ecclesiastical communion" (CCEO c. 192, §3).

Unlike some Western nations, where gypsies and nomads have often been neglected, the Eastern Christian regions, with a great deal of affinity for the culture of these newcomers, have generously welcomed them and offered a warm-hearted hospitality. In this way, the Eastern Catholic Churches are moved in justice to involve their ecclesial structures in the pastoral care of the entire Church.

Besides its general norms on the sacraments, most of all on *communicatio in sacris* and mixed marriages, with due adaptation to people on the move, the Eastern code provides for the spiritual needs of these faithful in cc. 192, §3 and 193, §2. With the magnitude of the "gypsy phenomenon" and its peculiarities, which do not always lend themselves to effective pastoral solutions (CIC c. 568), it is hoped that a more appropriate and long-lasting solution – always in concert with local ecclesial authorities – be developed from the pastoral structures contained in the Church's legislation and praxis.

The Latin code, among these structures, lists the Personal Prelature (CIC cc. 294-297), which could lead to a "Personal Prelature for People on the Move." Eastern Catholic hierarchs could refer, with due adaptation, to the norms of the Eastern code on the pastoral care of the Eastern Catholic faithful in territories where there is no hierarchy of their own Churches *sui iuris*. The phenomenon of the gypsies and nomads in the world highlights its diversity and specificity from one place to another and from a local Church to another.

Indulgences

Canon 992 of the Latin code defines an indulgence as the remission before God of temporal punishment for sins whose guilt is already forgiven. The faithful Christian who is duly disposed gains the indulgence under certain and defined conditions for either himself/herself or the departed. Indulgences are granted through the ministry of the Church which, as dispenser of the grace of redemption, distributes the treasury of the merits of Christ and the saints. Book Four of the Latin code, *On the Sanctifying Function of the Church*, devotes six canons exclusively to this topic (CIC cc. 992-997).

The Eastern code, on the other hand, does not even mention indulgences. It is not part of the Eastern tradition. Nevertheless, Eastern Christian faithful may profitably gain indulgences in accordance with the *Enchiridion Indulgentiarum* promulgated by the Apostolic Penitentiary on July 16, 1999. All Catholics who are duly disposed can gain indulgences for themselves or the departed. To be capable of gaining indulgences, a person must be baptized, not excommunicated, and in the state of grace. Eastern faithful can gain these spiritual favors (indulgences) granted through the ministry of the Latin Church. In addition, Eastern patriarchs and major archbishops enjoy the faculty of granting partial indulgences to the faithful of their own Churches everywhere (*Enchiridion Indulgentiarum*, n. 9).

Migration of Non-Christians to the West

The endless migration of people, particularly from the Near and Far East, to the various Christian regions of the West not only engages the hosting government agencies, but also the local Churches in promoting the pastoral care needed by the newcomers. The Church's pastoral care among migrant peoples is truly a missionary work. The Eastern code exhorts the eparchial bishop "to consider the non-baptized as being committed to him in the Lord and see that the love of Christ shines upon them from the witness of the Christian faithful living in ecclesiastical communion" (CCEO c. 192, §3).

In this regard, the Eastern Catholic Churches are involving their ministerial structures in the pastoral solicitude of the universal Church. Besides the basic sacramental norms, particularly *communicatio in sacris*, the Eastern code, with due adaptation for migrants, offers ecclesial structures for their pastoral care when it refers to the solicitude of the bishop towards the various groups of people in his territory (CCEO cc. 192, §3; 193, §2).

The Latin method of appointing diocesan or inter-diocesan chaplains is not always successful in addressing the *migratory phenomenon* and its special pastoral challenges. A comprehensive solution is needed that will find among the Church's various pastoral structures a way of balancing the autonomy of these unique groups with the responsibilities of local ecclesial authorities. One of the Latin structures that can do this is the Personal Prelature (cc. 294-297), possibly establishing a "Personal Prelature for Migrants." Local authorities of the Eastern Catholic Churches could have recourse, with due adaptation, to these norms in territories where their faithful are without their own shepherds. In this type of pastoral care it is advisable to follow the ecclesiology of the local Church that has developed effective ways of caring for various groups. Migration is a worldwide phenomenon, but it varies considerably in individual situations, from place to place, from local Church to local Church.

Non-Catholics

Sense of the term

Both codes (CCEO and CIC) commonly use the term *non-Catholic* to identify Christian faithful, Orthodox and Protestant, who are not in full communion with the Catholic Church. The term *Orthodox* is generally used to indicate the non-Catholic Oriental Churches that accept the ecumenical decisions of the Councils of Ephesus (431) and Chalcedon (451). Recently, however, this term, for historical reasons, has also been applied to the ancient Oriental Churches that did not accept some dogmatic formulas of one or of the other of the two aforementioned councils (UR 13).

Origin

In the early history of the one and only Church of God, there were certain rifts; because of various dissents, large communities separated from the full communion of the Catholic Church, sometimes not without human fault on both sides. The first divisions occurred in the East, whether because of opposition to the dogmatic formulas of the Councils of Ephesus and Chalcedon, or, later on, because of the separation of ecclesiastical communion between the Eastern patriarchates and the Roman See. Other divisions originated, after more than four centuries, in the West, because of the events that are commonly referred to as the Reformation. Since then, several ecclesiastical communities, national or confessional, have separated from the Roman See. Among those in which Catholic traditions and structures continue to subsist, at least partially, the Anglican Communion holds a special place.

The Second Vatican Council's Decree on Ecumenism, *Unitatis redintegratio*, addressing these non-Catholic Churches and Ecclesial Communities, neither ignores their situations nor dismisses the ties that, despite the division, continue to exist. In order to promote prudent ecumenism, the document puts forth the following considerations: First of all, the council declares explicitly that "those who are now born into these communities and who are brought up in the faith of Christ cannot be accused of the sin involved in the separation, and the Catholic Church looks upon them as brothers and sisters, with respect and love. For those who believe in Christ and were baptized are in some kind of communion with the Catholic Church, even though imperfect. The differences that exist in varying degrees between them and the Catholic Church, whether in doctrine and sometimes in discipline, or concerning the structure of the Church, do indeed create many obstacles, sometimes serious, to   full ecclesiastical communion. The ecumenical movement is striving to overcome these obstacles" (UR 3).

Non-Catholics are not Bound by Catholic Laws

Both codes (CCEO and CIC) often refer to non-Catholics in their relationships with the Catholic faithful. They declare explicitly that they are not bound by the merely ecclesiastical laws of the Catholic Church (CCEO c. 1490; CIC c. 11), but, obviously, by the divine, natural or positive law, to which all men and women are subject.

See *Baptism (Orthodox and Protestant)*.

Observance of the Proper Rite

The Vatican II Council' Decree on the Eastern Churches states: "Each and every Catholic as well as baptized members of any non-Catholic Church or community coming to the fullness of the Catholic communion should keep, follow and as far as possible observe their own rite (*retineant ritum et observent*) everywhere in the world" (OE 4). Consequently, Latin bishops should see to it that the Eastern faithful residing in their dioceses observe faithfully the ritual traditions of their own Church and favor the relations with the higher authority of their Church *sui iuris*. This implies vigilance on their part, especially in sacramental matters, always keeping in mind the different disciplines and the particular law to which these faithful are subject. The old principle of *locus regit actum* (when a legal transaction complies with the legal formalities of the country where it takes place, it is also valid in the country where it is to be given effect) does not apply in this matter.

The Eastern code concurs with the above conciliar assertion when c. 40, §3 states: "Also, the other Christian faithful are to foster the knowledge and appreciation of their own rite and are bound to observe it everywhere unless an exception is provided by the law." A *rite* is a liturgical, theological, spiritual and disciplinary heritage, differentiated by the culture and the circumstances of the history of peoples, which is expressed by each Church *sui iuris* in its own manner of living the Christian faith (CCEO c. 28). "The rites of the Eastern Churches, as the patrimony of the whole Church of Christ in which shines forth the tradition coming down from the Apostles through the Fathers, and which, in its variety, affirms the divine unity of the Catholic faith, are to be observed and promoted conscientiously" (CCEO c. 39).

In order to promote and safeguard observance of one's proper rite, the Eastern code c. 31 states: "No one is to presume to induce in any way the Christian faithful to transfer to another Church *sui iuris*." Furthermore: "A person who, ascribed to any Church *sui iuris*, including the Latin Church, and exercising an office, a ministry or another function in the Church, has presumed to induce any member of the Christian faithful whatsoever to transfer to another Church *sui iuris* is to be punished with an appropriate penalty (*congrua poena puniatur*)" (CCEO c. 1465). This Eastern code canon , although not found in the Latin code, expresses the legislator's will to protect the Eastern faithful wherever they may be from such attempts. Thus, the above norm should not be viewed as a simple exhortation but as a serious injunction, applying in a special way to bishops and religious superiors of the Latin Church.

Pastoral Care of Eastern Christians in Latin Dioceses

Eastern Diaspora
The juridical status of Eastern Catholics without a domicile or quasi-domicile in territories where they lack their own parish priest or in places where not even an Eastern hierarchy has been constituted is not a theoretical problem but a real one. In fact, the increasing phenomenon of groups from the Eastern Churches migrating to Europe, the United States, Australia, Canada, and South America calls for a study of the pastoral and canonical consequences of their more consistent presence in Latin dioceses. The inverse phenomenon, that is, of Latin faithful in Eastern territories, does not raise similar questions, because in the east for centuries there has been a long tradition of Latin dioceses and the pastoral care of the Latin faithful.

The ongoing migration of groups of Eastern Catholics to western countries has as a consequence that these faithful usually find themselves in a territory under the jurisdiction of a Latin bishop, while the Latin faithful in eastern territories usually has their own Latin ordinary. This is a legal and pastoral problem that is regulated by the CCEO and the CIC.

Vatican II Teaching

The Decree on the Pastoral Office of Bishops in the Church, *Christus Dominus*, states: "Where there are faithful of a different rite, the diocesan bishop should make provision either through priests or parishes of the same rite or through an episcopal vicar with the appropriate faculties and, where circumstances call for it, with episcopal rank. Alternatively, the diocesan bishop himself may exercise the function of ordinary for different rites" (CD 23). The same decree asserts that "the diocesan bishop can appoint one or more episcopal vicars who in virtue of their office enjoy the same power as common law confers on a vicar general in a clearly defined part of the diocese, or in a specific area of business, or in respect of the faithful of a particualr rite" (CD 27).

Latin Bishop and Pastor for Eastern Faithful

The Christian faithful, in virtue of their domicile or quasi-domicile, are committed to the care of the hierarch of the place and the pastor of the Church *sui iuris* to which they are ascribed. The Eastern code c. 38 regulates the condition of Eastern faithful without a pastor or hierarch of their own Church *sui iuris* by stating that they, "even if committed to the care of a hierarch or pastor of another Church *sui iuris*, nevertheless remain ascribed in their own Church *sui iuris*."

Canon 916, §§4-5 states: "If there is no pastor for the Christian faithful of a certain Church *sui iuris*, the eparchial bishop for those same faithful is to designate the pastor of another Church *sui iuris*, who is to assume their care as their proper pastor, with the consent, however, of the eparchial bishop of the pastor to be designated. In places where not even an exarchy has been erected for the Christian faithful of a certain Church *sui iuris*, the local hierarch of another Church *sui iuris*, even the Latin Church, is to be considered as the proper hierarch of these faithful, with due regard for canon 101. If, however, there are several local hierarchs, that one whom the Holy See has designated is to be considered as their proper hierarch or, if it concerns the Christian faithful of a certain patriarchal Church, the one whom the patriarch has designated with the assent of the Holy See."

Case in Point

The first issue occurs in territories where an Eastern hierarchy has been established inside or outside of the boundaries of the territory of an Eastern Church *sui iuris*, but a pastor for an Eastern community has not been appointed in that place. The solution offered by §4 is the possibility for their eparchial bishop of designating a pastor of another Church *sui iuris*, even of the Latin Church, if there is one in that place, who canonically takes care of them as their proper pastor. Of course, the consent of the eparchial bishop of the pastor to be designated must be in place.

The second issue occurs in territories where an Eastern hierarchy for the Christian faithful of a certain Church *sui iuris* has not yet been established, especially outside of the boundaries of the Church's territory. Within the territory of a patriarchal Church, in places where neither an Eastern eparchy nor an exarchy has been erected, the patriarch has the same rights and obligations as an eparchial bishop for those faithful (CCEO c. 101). Outside of the territory of an Eastern Church *sui iuris*, if there is only one bishop with jurisdiction, the hierarch for the Eastern faithful is the local hierarch of another Church *sui iuris*, even of the Latin Church.

For example, in a western country where there is no hierarchy for a particular Eastern Church *sui iuris,* the proper hierarch for the Eastern faithful is the local Latin bishop. If, in a western country, an Eastern hierarchy is present along with the Latin one, but there is no hierarchy of a particular Eastern community, the proper hierarch for those faithful is the Latin bishop or the Eastern hierarch designated by the Holy See, or, if those Christian faithful belong to a patriarchal or major archiepiscopal Church, designated by the patriarch or major archbishop with the assent of the Holy See. In the same place if, besides a Latin bishop, an Eastern hierarch has been appointed for a particular Church *sui iuris*, e.g., the Ukrainian Church, and another Eastern community, e.g., the Ethiopian Church, is present without its own hierarch, then it is up to the Holy See to choose one of the two bishops to serve as hierarch for these faithful. If, however, they belong to a patriarchal or major archiepiscopal Church, e.g., the Melkite or Malabar Churches, it is up to the patriarch or the major archbishop, with the assent of the Holy See, to assign them a proper hierarch.

Therefore, Eastern faithful, whose domicile or quasi-domicile is located in territories of the Latin Church and have no hierarchy of their own, are canonically subject to the Latin bishop, but they do not automatically fall under the pastoral care of the local pastor.

Latin Norm

In compliance with the teaching of Vatican II, the Latin code c. 383, §§1-2 states: "In exercising the function of a pastor, a diocesan bishop is to show himself concerned for all Christian faithful entrusted to his care, of whatever age, condition, or nationality they are, whether living in the territory or staying there temporarily; he is also to extend an apostolic spirit to those who are not able to make sufficient use of ordinary pastoral care because of the condition of their life and to those who no longer practice their religion. If he has faithful of different rites in his diocese, he is to provide for their spiritual needs either through priests or parishes of the same rite or through an episcopal vicar." This episcopal vicar possesses the same ordinary power which a vicar general has by universal law, according to the norm of the canons (c. 476).

Canon 518, having mentioned the principle of territoriality of a parish, states that "when it is expedient, personal parishes are to be established determined by reason of the rite." These personal ritual parishes are canonically part of the Latin diocese, and the pastors of the same rite are part of the Latin diocesan presbyterium. Nevertheless, the faithful of these personal parishes always remain ascribed in their own Eastern Church *sui iuris*.

"Christian faithful of Eastern Churches, even if committed to the care of a hierarch or pastor of another Church *sui iuris*, nevertheless remain ascribed in their own Church *sui iuris*" (CCEO c. 38).

Moreover, it would be opportune that the Latin bishop, before establishing a personal parish with a pastor or even an episcopal vicar for the care of Eastern faithful, consults the Congregation for the Eastern Churches and the respective hierarchy of the faithful. Eparchial bishops who appoint such priests are to draw up a plan in consultation with their respective patriarchs or major archbishops. If the latter agree, they are to act on their own authority and inform the competent dicastery of the Holy See (CCEO c. 193, §3; CIC c. 19).

"The Christian faithful of any Church *sui iuris,* even the Latin Church, who by reason of their office, ministry, or function have frequent dealings with the Christian faithful of another Church *sui iuris*, are to have an accurate formation in the knowledge and practice of the rite of the same Church in keeping with the importance of the office, ministry or function they hold" (CCEO c. 41).

See *Territorial or Personal Parish; Eparchy (Diocese).*

Pastors/Parish Priests

Requirement for His Nomination

For a presbyter to be named pastor (*parochus*), he must be of good morals, sound in doctrine, zealous for souls, and endowed with prudence and the other virtues and qualities required by law in order to fulfill the parochial ministry in a praiseworthy manner. If the presbyter is married, good morals are required of his wife and his children who live with him. The eparchial bishop, after having weighed all the circumstances, is to confer a vacant parish, without any partiality, on one whom he judges suitable. To make a judgment concerning a person's suitability he is to listen to the protopresbyter (vicar forane), conduct appropriate inquiries and, if he considers it opportune, listen to other Christian faithful as well, especially clerics (CCEO c. 285).

Right of Appointing

The right to name pastors belongs solely to the eparchial bishop, who appoints them freely. To entrust a parish to a member of a religious institute or society of common life in the manner of religious, the major superior proposes a suitable priest of his institute or society to the eparchial bishop for appointment, with due regard for agreements entered into with the eparchial bishop or other authority determined by the particular law of the respective Church *sui iuris.*

The pastor is permanent in his office; therefore he is not to be appointed for a limited period of time unless one of the following is applicable: 1° he is a member of a religious institute or society of common life in the manner of religious; 2° he agrees to this in writing; 3° it is a special situation, in which case the consent of the college of eparchial consultors is required; 4° the particular law of his Church *sui iuris* permit it (CCEO c. 284, §3).

Appointment of Eastern Pastor in a Latin Diocese and Vice Versa
These are the two anticipated cases:

1. Appointment for the pastoral care of the Eastern faithful of a personal parish in a Latin diocese. In this case, the bishops who appoint such presbyters, pastors or syncelli for the care of the Christian faithful of patriarchal or major archiepiscopal Churches are to draw up a plan in consultation with the respective patriarchs or major archbishops. If the latter agree, they are to act on their own authority and inform the Holy See as soon as possible; should the patriarchs or major archbishops disagree for whatever reason, the matter is to be referred to the Holy See (CCEO c. 193).
2. Appointment of an Eastern priest legitimately transferred or ascribed (incardinated) in a Latin diocese.

It is permissible to appoint a Latin priest as a pastor in an Eastern eparchy. Latin priests who are exercise their ministry in an Eastern Church, as well as Eastern priests in the Latin Church, must obtain from the Holy See the adaptation of rite or at least the faculty of bi-ritualism.

See *Adaptation of Rite; Biritualism; Celibacy and Married State of Eastern Clerics.*

Patriarchal Procurator at the Holy See

A patriarch or major archbishop can have a procurator (*apocrysarius*) at the Holy See appointed personally by him with the prior assent of the Roman Pontiff (CCEO c. 61). His role is to settle the patriarch's matters before the various dicasteries of the Roman Curia. As a rule, this title is given to a cleric and his duties may be varied as well as sensitive, according to the needs and circumstances.

Pious Unions

The 1917 Pio-Benedictine Code of Canon Law (c. 707) and the 1957 Motu Proprio *Cleri Sanctitati* (c. 553) offered the following description: "Associations of the faithful that are erected for the exercise of some pious or charitable work come by the name *pious union.*" The current legislation addresses religious institutes such as monasteries *sui iuris*, orders and congregations (CCEO cc.410-553), societies of common life according to the manner of religious (cc. 554-562), secular institutes (cc. 563-569), and other forms of consecrated life and societies of apostolic life (cc. 570-572). Canons 18 and 26 deal with the rights of the Christian faithful to found and to direct associations that serve charitable and pious purposes or that promote the

Christian vocation in the world; also, ecclesiastical authority has the authority to regulate them in view of the common good. Similar norms are found in the canons 215 and 223 of the Latin code.

Protosyncellus and Syncelli/Vicar General and Episcopal Vicars

Office

In each eparchy a protosyncellus/vicar general is to be appointed who, endowed with ordinary vicarious power in accord with the norm of common law, assists the eparchial bishop in governing the whole eparchy (CCEO c. 245; CIC c. 475, §1). As often as the good governance of the eparchy requires it, one or several syncelli/episcopal vicars can be appointed, who have by virtue of the law itself the same authority as that attributed to the protosyncellus/vicar general but limited to a given section of the eparchy, or to certain kinds of affairs, or for the Christian faithful ascribed to another Church *sui iuris*, or for a certain group of persons (CCEO c. 246; CIC c. 476).

Appointment

The protosyncellus and the syncelli are freely appointed by the eparchial bishop and can freely be removed by him. They are to be celibate presbyters, unless the particular law of their Church *sui iuris* has established otherwise; if possible, they should be from the clerics ascribed to the eparchy, not less than thirty years of age, have a doctorate, licentiate or expertise in some sacred science, and commendable for sound doctrine, uprightness, prudence and practical experience (CCEO c. 247, §2).

The eparchial bishop is permitted to take the protosyncellus or syncelli from another eparchy, or from another Church *sui iuris*, with the consent of their eparchial bishop. In the strict sense of the term, it would not be contrary to law to appoint a Latin priest as a protosyncellus. In such a case, the Latin protosyncellus remains incardinated into the Latin Church and should obtain an indult of bi-ritualism from the Holy See.

A coadjutor bishop must be appointed protosyncellus of his eparchy; if there is no coadjutor, the eparchial bishop should appoint the auxiliary bishop as protosyncellus (CCEO c. 215, §§1-2).

Quinquennial Report

The eparchial bishop of any Church *sui iuris*, including the Latin Church, is to inform the Holy See on the occasion of the quinquennial report, about the state and needs of the Christian faithful who, even if they are ascribed into another Church *sui iuris*, are committed to his pastoral care (CCEO c. 399, §1; CIC c. 339, §1).

Territorial or Personal Parish

Both codes contemplate the founding of personal parishes by reason of the rite of the faithful. As a rule, a parish is territorial, that is, it embraces all the Christian faithful of a certain area. If, however, the eparchial bishop, after consulting the presbyteral council, judges it advisable, personal parishes are to be erected, by reason of nationality, of language, of ascription of the Christian faithful (*ascriptionis christifidelium*) to another Church *sui iuris*, or indeed of some other clearly distinguishing factor (CCEO c. 280, §1).

The Latin code has a similar norm: "As a general rule a parish is to be territorial, that is, one which includes all the Christian faithful of a certain territory. When it expedient, however, personal parishes are to be established determined by reason of rite (*ratione ritus*), language, or nationality of the Christian faithful of some territory, or even for some other reason" (CIC c. 518).

The establishment of personal parishes is not always feasible:

- In a Latin diocese there might be several groups, more or less numerous, of faithful belonging to different Eastern Churches *sui iuris*;
- Eastern priests may not be readily available to assume their pastoral care;
- Sufficient resources may be lacking to establish such parishes.

In these and similar cases, the eparchial bishop should appoint an episcopal vicar with the same authority as the vicar general "for all the rites" present in his diocese (a multi-ritual and multi-lingual delegate).

Visitor for Eastern Faithful

Apostolic Visitator

In territories where the Eastern faithful do not possess their own hierarchy, the Holy See shows its solicitude towards them through visitators and delegates. When these clerics are of papal appointment they are called "apostolic visitators." A visitator or delegate carries out his function in accordance with the procedure laid down *ad hoc* by his decree of appointment. As a rule, he verifies the state and needs of the faithful, encouraging them, meeting with the local bishops, and making a report with proposals to the Congregation for the Eastern Churches. A different procedure is currently followed in Belorussia and Kazakhstan where, in collaboration with the Latin ordinaries, the prelates delegated by the Holy See care for these faithful with specific acts of governance.

Patriarchal Visitators

Patriarchal power can be exercised validly only within the territorial boundaries of the patriarchal Church. However, it is the right and the obligation of a patriarch to seek appropriate information concerning the Christian faithful who reside outside the territorial boundaries of the Church over which he presides, something that he can do through a visitator sent by him with the assent of the Holy See. Before he begins his function, the visitator must present his letter of appointment to the eparchial bishop of those faithful.

When the visitation is completed, he is to send a report to the patriarch, who, after discussing the matter in the synod of bishops, can propose suitable measures to the Holy See; these proposals are to provide for the protection and enhancement of the spiritual good of the Christian faithful of the Church over which he presides, wherever they may be, even through the erection of parishes and exarchies or eparchies for them (CCEO c. 148).

TABLE A: CATHOLIC CHURCHES *SUI IURIS*

The following are the Catholic Churches *sui iuris*, each belonging to one of various Ritual Traditions:

Patriarchal Churches:

Armenian Church	Ritual Tradition: Armenian
Chaldean Church	Ritual Tradition: Chaldean
Coptic Church	Ritual Tradition: Alexandrian
Maronite Church	Ritual Tradition: Antiochian
Melkite Church	Ritual Tradition: Byzantine
Syriac Church	Ritual Tradition: Antiochian

Major Archiepiscopal Churches

Ukrainian Church	Ritual Tradition: Byzantine
Syro-Malabar Church	Ritual Tradition: Chaldean
Syro-Malankara Church	Ritual Tradition: Antiochian
Romanian Church	Ritual Tradition: Byzantine

Metropolitan Churches Sui Iuris

Ethiopian Church	Ritual Tradition: Alexandrian
Ruthenian Church	Ritual Tradition: Byzantine
Slovak Church	Ritual Tradition: Byzantine

Eparchial and Other Churches Sui Iuris

Albanian Church	Ritual Tradition: Byzantine
Belarussian Church	Ritual Tradition: Byzantine
Bulgarian Church	Ritual Tradition: Byzantine
Hellenic Church	Ritual Tradition: Byzantine
Hungarian Church	Ritual Tradition: Byzantine
Italo-Albanian Church	
a.k.a. Italo-Greek Church	Ritual Tradition: Byzantine
Krizevci Church	
a.k.a. Yugoslav Church	Ritual Tradition: Byzantine
Russian Church	Ritual Tradition: Byzantine

TABLE B: EASTERN CATHOLIC CHURCHES IN USA

The following are the established Eastern hierarchies in the United States and Eastern parishes without an established hierarchy.

Eastern Hierarchies

Ruthenian Catholic Church *Sui Iuris*
Four eparchies: Metropolitan Archeparchy of Pittsburgh, PA; Eparchies in Passaic, NJ, Parma, OH, and Van Nuys, CA (Eparchial bishop resides in Phoenix, AZ).

Ukrainian Catholic Church
Four eparchies: Metropolitan Archeparchy of Philadelphia, PA; Eparchies in Stamford, CT; Parma, OH; and Chicago, IL.

Melkite Catholic Church
One eparchy: Newton, MA.

Romanian Catholic Church
One eparchy: Canton, OH.

Armenian Catholic Church
One eparchy for USA and Canada: Brooklyn, NY.

Chaldean Catholic Church
Two eparchies: Detroit, MI; San Diego, CA.

Maronite Catholic Church
Two eparchies: Brooklyn, NY; Los Angeles, CA (Eparchial bishop resides in St. Louis, MO).

Syriac Catholic Church
One eparchy for USA and Canada: Union City, NJ.

Syro-Malabar Catholic Church
One eparchy: Chicago, IL.

None of the other Eastern Catholic Churches has an established hierarchy as yet in the USA.

Parishes without their own hierarchies

Russian Catholic Church
Three parishes: San Francisco, CA; Los Angeles, CA; New York City, NY.

Italo-Greek Catholic Church
Two parishes: New York City, NY; Las Vegas, NV.

Coptic Catholic Church
Two parishes: New York City, NY; Los Angeles, CA.

Syro-Malankara Catholic Church
Twelve chapels in the USA and Canada.

Slovak Catholic Church
In the USA these Byzantine Catholics are not distinguished from Ruthenian Catholics, much as Ruthenians are not distinguished from Ukrainian Catholics in Canada. However, there is a Slovak Eparchy in Toronto for all of Canada.

Hungarian Catholic Church
A few parishes: all of them are part of the Ruthenian eparchies.

Belarussian Catholic Church
One parish: Chicago, IL.

INDEX OF TERMS

SACRAMENTS OF INITIATION AND ASCRIPTION, 9-27

MATRIMONIAL ISSUES, 28-41

ORDINATION, 41-48

Corresponding Terms in CCEO and CIC

CCEO	CIC
Ascription (as cleric)	Incardination
Apostolic Exarch	Apostolic Vicar
Apostolic Exarchy or Exarchate	Apostolic Vicariate
Assembly of Hierarchs	Episcopal Conference
Blessing of Marriage	Assisting at Marriage
Church *sui iuris*	Ritual Church
Common Law	Common Law
Chrismation with Holy Myron	Confirmation
Commemoration (Divine Liturgy)	Commemoration (Holy Mass)
Divine Eucharist	Most Holy Eucharist
Divine Liturgy	Holy Mass
Divine Praises	Liturgy of the Hours
Eparchial Assembly	Diocesan Synod
Eparchial Bishop	Diocesan Bishop
Eparchial Curia/Chancery	Diocesan Curia/Chancery
Eparchy	Diocese
Hierarch	Ordinary
Hierarch of the Place	Ordinary of the Place
Major Archbishop	_____
Major Archiepiscopal Church	_____
Major Excommunication	Excommunication
Metropolitan of a Patriarchal Church	_____
Metropolitan *Sui Iuris*	_____
Metropolitan Church *Sui Iuris*	_____
Minor Excommunication	Interdict/Suspension
Myron	Chrism
Particular Law	Particular Law
Patriarchal Assembly	_____
Patriarchal Church	_____
Permanent Synod	_____

144

CCEO	CIC
Protoprebyter	Vicar Forane
Protosyncellus	Vicar General
Statutes	Statutes/Ordinances
Stauropegiac Monastery	
Synaxis	Chapter
Syncellus	Episcopal Vicar
Synod of Bishops of a Patriarchal Church	
Transfer (of cleric)	Excardination/Incardination
Typicon	Statutes/Constitution

FORMS OF RESCRIPTS BY THE EASTERN CONGREGATION

ADMISSION TO THE NOVITIATE IN THE RELIGIOUS INSTITUTE OF ANOTHER RITE

Beatissime Pater,

.... fidelis Ecclesiae .... Dioeceseos/Eparchiae
................., humiliter petit ut in .... ad novitiatum
admitti possit et, praescripto tempore, in eodem Instituto religiosam professionem
emittere valeat, ritui .... sese conformando.

* * *

Congregatio pro Ecclesiis Orientalibus, vigore facultatum a Summo Pontifice
Benedicto PP. XVI sibi tributarum, benigne concedit ut Orator in Instituto de quo in
precibus ad novitiatum et ad religiosam professionem admitti possit.

Eidem Oratori fit insuper facultas sese in omnibus conformandi ritui
......................., ea tamen lege ut ritui propriae Ecclesiae *sui iuris* adscriptus maneat,
eundemque sequi debeat, si, quacumque de causa, ad nuper dictum Institutum pertinere
desierit.

Contrariis quibuslibet non obstantibus.

Datum Romae, ex Aedibus Congregationis pro Ecclesiis Orientalibus,

die ....

ADMISSION OF A LAY ORTHODOX PERSON TO THE LATIN CHURCH

Beatissime Pater,

..................................., fidelis Ecclesiae Orthodoxae .... cupiens ad
plenam communionem cum Ecclesia Catholica pervenire, petit - ad normam can. 35
CCEO - ut ritui latino ascribi possit.

Ordinarius latinus preces commendat.

* * *

Congregatio pro Ecclesiis Orientalibus vigore facultatum a Summo Pontifice
Benedicto PP. XVI sibi tributarum, attentis precibus ac omnibus mature perpensis,
benigne concedit Oratori ut emittens professionem fidei catholicae ritui latino ascribi
valeat, ceterum servatis de iure servandis.

Contrariis quibuslibet minime obstantibus.

Datum Romae, ex Aedibus Congregationis pro Ecclesiis Orientalibus,

die ....

DISPENSATION FROM VOWS OF RELIGIOUS CLERICS

Beatissime Pater,

.... professus a votis perpetuis .... in Ordine..............., humiliter petit dispensationem ab iisdem votis, ob causas expositas.

Moderator   Generalis   preces   commendat   et   Episcopus .... in Eparchiam/Dioecesim Oratorem recipit.

*   *   *

Congregatio pro Ecclesiis Orientalibus, vigore facultatum a Summo Pontifice Benedicto PP. XVI sibi tributarum, omnibus perpensis, petitam dispensationem concedit, iuxta preces, ita ut Orator maneat liberatus a votis ceterisque obligationibus suae   professionis   religiosae   atque   in   Eparchiam/Dioecesim .... rite tamquam clericus ascribatur.

Contrariis quibuslibet minime obstantibus.

Datum Romae, ex Aedibus Congregationis pro Ecclesiis Orientalibus,

die...

DISPENSATION FROM VOWS OF RELIGIOUS NON-CLERICS

Beatissime Pater,

...., professus votorum perpetuorum in Congregatione ...., humiliter petit dispensationem ab iisdem votis, ob causas expositas.

Moderator Generalis preces commendat.

*   *   *

Congregatio pro Ecclesiis Orientalibus, vigore facultatum a Summo Pontifice Benedicto PP. XVI sibi tributarum, omnibus perpensis, petitam dispensationem concedit, iuxta preces, ita ut Orator maneat liberatus a votis ceterisque obligationibus suae professionis religiosae et separatus a sua Religione atque, deposita forma habitus religiosi, tamquam simplex laicus habeatur, servatis tamen ceteris de iure servandis.

Nisi ab Oratori infra decem dies a recepta communicatione acceptetur, praesens Rescriptum quamcumque vim amittit.

Contrariis quibuslibet minime obstantibus.

Datum Romae, ex Aedibus Congregationis pro Ecclesiis Orientalibus,

die ....

ERECTION OF AN EASTERN HOUSE OF A LATIN RELIGIOUS INSTITUTE

Beatissime Pater,

.... Superior Generalis Congregationis ...., ritus latini, humiliter poscit beneplacitum apostolicum ad domum religiosam apud Civitatem..........., Ecclesiae .... ad normam iuris adscriptam constituendam iuxta Decretum Conciliare de Ecclesiis Orientalibus Catholicis n. 6, necnon can. 432 Codicis Canonum Ecclesiarum Orientalium.

Hierarcha loci consentit ac preces commendat.

* * *

Congregatio pro Ecclesiis Orientalibus, vigore facultatum a Summo Pontifice Benedicto PP. XVI sibi tributarum, omnibus bene perpensis, gratiam petitam benigne largitur, ita ut supradicta domus ad Ecclesiam .... adscriptam erigatur, quae ritum liturgicum ac ius canonicum Ecclesiae .... servare debeat eiusdem Hierarchiae ad normam iuris subiciatur, servatis tamen praescriptis statutorum quae internum regimen supradictae domus respiciunt necnon privilegiis eidem Instituto a Sede Apostolica concessis.

Contrariis qiubuslibet minime obstantibus.

Datum Romae, ex Aedibus Congregationis pro Ecclesiis Orientalibus,

die ....

EXCLAUSTRATION OF RELIGIOUS CLERICS

Beatissime Pater,

....................., Presbyter professus votorum perpetuorum ...., ob causas expositas humiliter petit indultum exclaustrationis sub dependentia Episcopi ...., qui eum in suam dioecesim acceptat.

* * *

Congregatio pro Ecclesiis Orientalibus, vigore facultatum a Summo Pontifice Benedicto PP. XVI, sibi tributarum, omnibus perpensis, concedit Oratori indultum vivendi extra claustra usque ad .... una cum dispensatione a regulis et obligationibus quae cum statu religiosi exclaustrati componi nequeunt.

Orator autem, exteriore forma habitus religiosi deposita, sub iurisdictione Ordinarii benevoli receptoris subiectus maneat eique, loco Superiorum propriae Religionis, etiam ratione voti, obedire tenetur, servatis ceteris de iure servandis.

Contrariis quibuslibet non obstantibus.

Datum Romae, ex Aedibus Congregationis pro Ecclesiis Orientalibus,

die ....

EXCLAUSTRATION OF RELIGIOUS NON-CLERICS

Beatissime Pater,

...., professus/professa a votis perpetuis Congregationis ...., humiliter implorat indultum exclaustrationis, ob causas expositas.

Superior Generalis preces commendat.

* * *

Congregatio pro Ecclesiis Orientalibus, vigore facultatum a Summo Pontifice Benedicto PP. XVI sibi tributarum, omnibus perpensis, concedit Oratori/Oratrici indultum vivendi extra claustra ad ...., una cum dispensatione a regulis et obligationibus quae cum statu exclaustrati/exclaustratae componi nequeunt.

Orator/Oratrix autem, exteriore forma habitus religiosi/religiosae deposita, Hierarchae proprii ritus territorii ubi commoratur, loco Superiorum propriae Religionis, etiam ratione voti, obedire tenetur, servatis de iure servandis.

Contrariis quibuslibet minime obstantibus.

Datum Romae, ex Aedibus Congregationis pro Ecclesiis Orientalibus,

die ....

FACULTY OF BI-RITUALISM

Beatissime Pater,

..........................., presbyter Dioeceseos/Eparchiae/Ordinis, ritus .... humiliter postulat, ut facultas sibi fiat Sacrum litandi atque cetera sacerdotalia munera ritu quoque ....obeundi.

Causa est: bonum spirituale fidelium ritus .... inter quos versatur.

* * *

Congregatio pro Ecclesiis Orientalibus, vigore facultatum quibus pollet ex concessione Summi Pontificis Benedicti PP. XVI, omnibus mature perpensis, gratiam petitam benigne largitur, iuxta preces, cauto tamen ut Orator de Hierarchae seu Ordinarii loci sententia, ritum .... scite didicerit, remoto quovis vel admirationis periculo et excluso omni illegitimo syncretismo liturgico, servatis ceteris de iure servandis.

Praesentibus ad .... valituris.

Contrariis quibuslibet non obstantibus.

Datum Romae, ex Aedibus Congregationis pro Ecclesiis Orientalibus,

die ....

RENEWAL OF THE FACULTY OF BI-RITUALISM

Beatissime Pater,

...., presbyter Dioeceseos/Eparchiae/Ordinis, ritus ....., humiliter petit renovationem facultatis, quam alias obtinuit Rescripto Congregationis pro Ecclesiis Orientalibus, die ...., Sacrum nempe litandi atque cetera sacerdotalia munera ritu quoque .... obeundi, iisdem perdurantibus causis.

* * *

Congregatio pro Ecclesiis Orientalibus, vigore facultatum quibus pollet ex concessione Summi Pontificis Benedicti PP. XVI, omnibus mature perpensis, gratiam petitam benigne largitur, iuxta preces, in forma et terminis praecedentis concessionis, ad ....

Datum Romae, ex Aedibus Congregationis pro Ecclesiis Orientalibus,

die ....

ORDINATION OF AN EASTERN CANDIDATE ACCORDING TO THE LATIN RITE

Beatissime Pater,

.............................., Ecclesiae .... alumnus Dioecesis/Eparchiae .... humiliter petit ut ad sacrum Diaconatus et Presbyteratus Ordinem ritu latino admitti possit, ob causas allatas; insuper, aliquando ordinatus, facultatem habeat Sacrum litandi atque cetera diaconalia, deinde sacerdotalia munera utroque ritu, ..., obeundi, iuxta bonum spirituale fidelium cuiuscumque ritus adstantium, inter quos versatur.

Episcopus .... preces commendat.

* * *

Congregatio pro Ecclesiis Orientalibus, vigore facultatum a Summo Pontifice Benedicto PP. XVI sibi tributarum, benigne concedit gratiam, iuxta preces, servatis de iure servandis, ea tamen lege ut Orator ritui .... adscriptus maneat.

Contrariis quibuslibet non obstantibus.

Datum Romae, ex Aedibus Congregationis pro Ecclesiis Orientalibus,

die ....

TRANSFER OF A LAY PERSON TO ANOTHER CHURCH *SUI IURIS*

Beatissime Pater,

.... ob rationes expositas petit indultum transeundi ab Ecclesia .... ad Ecclesiam ....

* * *

Congregatio pro Ecclesiis Orientalibus, vigore facultatum a Summo Pontifice Benedicto PP. XVI sibi tributarum, attentis precibus ac omnibus mature perpensis, concedit Oratori indultum transitus ab Ecclesia .... ad Ecclesiam ....ad omnes iuris effectus.

Transitus ad novam Ecclesiam vim habebit a momento quo Orator coram dictae Ecclesiae parocho vel Hierarcha intra eorundem territorii fines – vel coram presbytero ab alterutro delegato – et duobus testibus, suam voluntatem novum ritum assumendi declaraverit.

Parochus vel Hierarcha, de quibus supra, sedulo curet:

1. Ut in libro baptizatorum novae paroeciae peractus transitus quam primum adnotetur;
2. Ut de peracto transitu nuntius mittatur ad baptismi parochum, cuius erit ritus mutationem in libro baptizatorum adnotare et de peracta adnotatione mittentem certiorem facere.
3. Filii infra decimum quartum aetatis annum expletum ipso iure ascribuntur novae Ecclesiae *sui iuris* patris vel matris, ad normam CCEO can. 34; singula tamen eorum nomina expresse adnotentur in libro baptizatorum paroeciae ritus "ad quem" una cum nomine patris vel, in mixtis nuptiis, matris.

Sex mensibus a die concessionis elapsis, praesens Rescriptum omnem vim amittit.

Datum Romae, ex Aedibus Congregationis pro Ecclesiis Orientalibus,

die ....

SELECT BIBLIOGRAPHY IN ENGLISH

BOOKS

Code of Canon Law. Latin-English Edition. Prepared under the Auspices of the CLSA. Washington: CLSA, 1998.

Code of Canons of the Eastern Churches. Latin-English Edition. Prepared under the Auspices of the CLSA. Washington: CLSA, 2002.

The Canon Law: Letter and Spirit. Prepared by the Canon Law Society of Great Britain and Ireland in Association with the Canadian Canon Law Society. Collegeville: Liturgical Press, 1995.

The Code of Canon Law: A Text and Commentary. Commissioned by the CLSA. Edited by James Coriden, Thomas Green, Donald Heintschel. New York: Paulist Press, 1885.

A New Commentary on the Code of Canon Law. Commissioned by the CLSA. Edited by John Beal, James Coriden, Thomas Green. New York: Paulist Press, 2000.

Code of Canon Law Annotated. Prepared under the Responsibility of the Instituto Martin de Azpilcueta of the University of Navarre and Edited by Ernest Caparros. Montreal: Wilson & Lafleur Limitée, 2004.

Exegetical Commentary on the Code of Canon Law. Prepared under the Responsibility of the Instituto Martin de Azpilcueta of the University of Navarre and Edited by Ernest Caparros. Montreal: Wilson & Lafleur Limitée, 2004.

A Guide to the Eastern Code: A Commentary on the CCEO. Edited by George Nedungatt. Rome: Pontificio Istituto Orientale, 2002.

CLSA Advisory Opinions 1984-1993. Edited by Patrick Cogan. Washington: CLSA, 1995.

CLSA Advisory Opinions 1994-2000. Edited by Arthur Espelage. Washington: CLSA, 2002.

CLSA Advisory Opinions 2001-2005. Edited by Arthur Espelage. Washington: CLSA 2006.

Comparative Sacramental Discipline in the CCEO and CIC: A Handbook for the Pastoral Care of Members of Other Catholic Churches Sui Iuris. Edited by Francis Marini. Washington: CLSA, 2003.

Ius Ecclesiarum Vehiculum Caritatis. Proceedings of the International Symposium for the Decennial of the CCEO. Prepared under the Auspices of the Congregation for the Eastern Churches by Silvano Agrestini and Danilo Ceccarelli Morolli. Rome: Vatican Library Press, 2004.

The Blackwell Dictionary of Eastern Christianity. Edited by Ken Parry *et al.* Oxford: Blackwell Publishers, 1989.

The Blackwell Companion to Eastern Christianity. Edited by Ken Parry *et al.* Oxford: Blackwell Publishers, 2007.

The Eastern Code: Text and Resources. Edited by Yoannis Gaid. Rome: Pontificio Istituto Orientale, 2007.

Jobe Abbass, *Two Codes in Comparison.* Rome: Pontificio Istituto Orientale, 1997.

_____, *The Consecrated Life: A Comparative Commentary of the Eastern and Latin Codes.* Ottawa: St. Paul University Press, 2008.

Kuriakose Bharanikulangara, *The Code of Canons of the Oriental Churches.* Alwaye: St. Thomas Academy, 1990.

_____, *Particular Law of the Eastern Catholic Churches.* New York: St. Maron Publications, 1996.

Jose Chiramel, *The Code of Canons of the Eastern Churches: A Study and Interpretation.* Alwaye: St. Thomas Academy, 1992.

John Faris, *Eastern Catholic Churches: Constitution and Governance.* New York: St. Maron Publications, 1992.

Edward Faulk, *101 Questions and Answers on Eastern Catholic Churches.* New York: Paulist Press, 2007.

John Huels, *The Pastoral Companion: A Canon Law Handbook for Catholic Ministry.* Chicago: Franciscan Press, 2002.

Walter Kasper, *A Handbook of Spiritual Ecumenism.* New York: New City Press, 2007.

Varghese Koluthara, *Rightful Autonomy of Religious Institutes: A Comparative Study.* Bangalore: Dharmaram Publications, 2005.

John Kochuthundil, *Reciprocal Rights and Obligations of the Eparchial Bishops and Presbyters.* New York: St. Maron Publications, 1998.

Xavier Koodapuzha, *Communion of Churches.* Kottayam: Oriental Institute Publications, 1993.

Wojciech Kowal-William Woestman, *Special Marriage Cases and Procedures.* Ottawa: St. Paul University Press, 2008.

David Motiuk, *Eastern Christians in the New World.* Ottawa: St. Paul University Press, 2005.

George Nedungatt, *Laity and Church Temporalities: Appraisal of a Tradition.* Bangalore: Institute of Oriental Studies, 2000.

Paul Pallath, *The Synod of Bishops of Catholic Oriental Churches.* Rome: St. Thomas Christian Fellowship, 1994.

_____, *Local Episcopal Bodies in East and West.* Kottayam: Oriental Institute Publications, 1997.

_____, *Catholic Eastern Churches: Heritage and Identity.* Rome: St. Thomas Christian Fellowship, 1994.

_____, *Church and Its Most Basic Element.* Rome: Herder Publications, 1995.

Jose Pulickal, *A Dictionary of Canon Law.* Manila: Logos Publications, 2005.

Victor Pospishil, *Eastern Catholic Church Law.* New York: Saint Maron Publications, 1996.

Jaroslav Skira, *Windows to the East.* Ottawa: Novalis Publications, 2001.

Michael Vattappalam, *The Congregation for the Eastern Churches: Origins and Competence.* Rome: Vatican Library Press, 1999.

Ivan Žužek, *Understanding the Eastern Code.* Rome: Pontificio Istituto Orientale, 1997.

ARTICLES

Jobe Abbass, *The Temporal Goods of the Church: A Comparative Study of the Two Codes,* Periodica 83 (1994) 669-714.

_____ , *Canonical Dispositions for the Care of Eastern Catholics outside Their Territory,* Periodica 86 (1997) 321-362.

_____, *Marriage in the Codes of Canon Law,* Apollinaris 68 (1995) 521-565.

_____, *The Inter-relationship of the Latin and Eastern Codes,* The Jurist 58 (1998) 1-40.

_____, *The Roman Rota and Appeals from Tribunals of the Eastern Patriarchal Churches,* Periodica 89 (2000) 439-490.

_____, *Latin Bishops' Duty of Care towards Eastern Catholics,* Studia Canonica 35 (2001) 7-31.

_____, *Associations of the Christian Faithful in the CIC and CCEO,* Apollinaris 73 (2000) 227-244.

_____, *Assemblies of Hierarchs for Eastern Catholic Bishops in the Diaspora,* Studia Canonica 40 (2006) 371-396.

Michel Aoun, *Matrimonium Contrahere or Matrimoniale Foedus Celebrare: The Peregrinations of the Conception of Marriage,* Revue de Droit Canonique 53 (2003) 213-226.

Peter Babie, *Australia's Ukrainian Catholics, Canon Law, and the Eparchial Statutes,* The Australasian Catholic Record 81 (2004) 32-48.

Roman Cholij, *An Eastern Catholic Married Clergy in North America: Recent Changes in Legal Status and Ecclesiological Perspective,* Studia Canonica 31 (1997) 311-340.

Patrick Connolly, *Contrasts in the Western and Eastern Approaches to Marriage,* Studia Canonica 35 (2001) 357-402.

James Coriden, *The Rights of Parishes,* Studia Canonica 28 (1994) 293-309.

_____, *The Vindication of Parish Rights,* The Jurist 54 (1994) 22-39.

Peter Erdo, *The Codification of the Law for Eastern Churches: Is It Latinization?* Revue de Droit Canonique 51 (2001) 323-333.

Michael Fahey, *On the CCEO and Orthodox-Catholic Reunion,* The Jurist 56 (1996) 456-464.

John Faris, *Pastoral Care of Migrants and the CCEO,* CLSA Proceedings 63 (2001) 85-99.

_____, *The Latin Church Sui Iuris,* The Jurist 62 (2002) 280-293.

_____, *Penal Law in the Catholic Churches: A Comparative Overview,* Folia Canonica 2 (1999) 53-93.

_____, *Territory and the Eastern Catholic Experience in the United States,* Folia Canonica 5 (2002) 51-58.

Robert Flummerfelt, *Theology of Marriage: Complementarity Between the Latin and Eastern Codes,* CLSA Proceedings 66 (2004) 13-25.

George Gallaro, *The Mystery of Crowning: An Inter-ecclesial Perspective,* CLSA Proceedings 51 (1989) 185-200.

_____, *The Eastern Code and the Latin Church,* The Australasian Catholic Record 69 (1992) 217-221.

_____, *The Ecumenical Dimension of Canon Law,* Eastern Churches Journal 2 (1995) 19-39.

_____, *The Bishop Emeritus: An Ecclesial Consideration,* The Jurist 66 (2006) 374-389.

George Gallaro-Dimitri Salachas, *Inter-ecclesial Matters in the Communion of Churches,* The Jurist 60 (2000) 256-309.

_____, *The 'Ritus Sacer' of the Sacrament of Marriage in the Byzantine Churches*, Studi sull' Oriente Cristiano 12 (2008) n.2, 83-110.

Thomas Green, *The Fostering of Ecumenism: Comparative Reflection on the Two Codes*, Periodica 85 (1996) 397-444.

_____, *Diocesan and Parish Structures: A Comparison of Selected Canons in the CIC and CCEO*, Studia Canonica 33 (1999) 349-397.

_____, *The Latin and Eastern Codes: Guiding Principles*, The Jurist 62 (2002) 235-279.

Sharon Holland, *A Spirit to Animate the Letter. CCEO Title XII*, The Jurist 56 (1996) 288-306.

John Huels, *Determining the Correct Canonical Rules for Ambiguous Administrative Acts*, Studia Canonica 37 (2003) 5-54.

Andrew Kania, *Breathing Deeply, with One Lung: The Problem with Latin Church Dominance within the Catholic Church*, The Australasian Catholic Record 81 (2004) 198-211.

Francis Marini, *The Adjudication of Inter-ritual Marriage Cases in the Tribunal*, Folia Canonica 2 (1999) 231-266.

Frederick McManus, *The Code of Canons of the Eastern Catholic Churches*, The Jurist 53 (1993) 22-61.

_____, *Marriage in the Canons of the Eastern Catholic Churches*, The Jurist 54 (1994) 56-80.

David Motiuk, *The CCEO: Some Ten Years Later*, Studia Canonica 36 (2002) 129-167.

George Nedungatt, *The Minister of the Sacrament of Marriage in the East and the West*, Periodica 90 (2001) 305-388.

_____, *Celibate and Married Clergy in CCEO Canon 373*, Studia Canonica 36 (2002) 129-167.

_____, *The Patriarchal Ministry in the Church of the First Millennium*, The Jurist 60 (2001) 1-89.

_____, *USA Forbidden Territory for Married Eastern Catholic Priests*, The Jurist 63 (2003) 139-170.

Antonio Pinheiro, *Religious Life in the Eastern Code*, Vidyajyoti 60 (1996) 606-617 & 663-671.

James Provost, *Some Practical Issues for Latin Canon Lawyers from the CCEO*, The Jurist 51 (1991) 38-66.